A Concise Guide to Canon Law

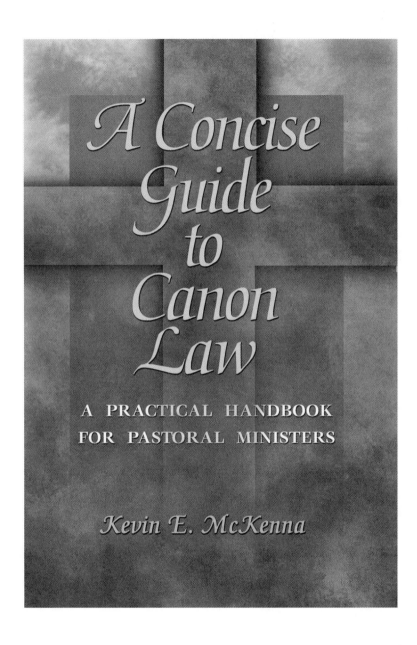

A Concise Guide to Canon Law

A PRACTICAL HANDBOOK FOR PASTORAL MINISTERS

Kevin E. McKenna

ave maria press   Notre Dame, Indiana

Nihil Obstat: Reverend William F. Laird, J.C.L.
                    Censor Deputatus

Imprimatur: The Most Reverend Matthew H. Clark
                    Bishop of Rochester

Given at Rochester, NY on 10 November 1999

Excerpts from the *Code of Canon Law, Latin-English Edition*, copyright 1999 by the Canon Law Society of America. Reprinted with permission.

Scripture texts in this work are taken from the *New American Bible with Revised New Testament and Revised Psalms* © 1991, 1986, 1970 Confraternity of Christian Doctrine, Washington, D.C., and are used by permission of the copyright owner. All Rights Reserved. No part of the *New American Bible* may be reproduced in any form without permission in writing from the copyright owner.

© 2000 by Ave Maria Press, Inc.

International Standard Book Number: 0-87793-934-9

Cover and text design by Katherine Robinson Coleman

Printed and bound in the United States of America.

Library of Congress Cataloging-in-Publication Data
McKenna, Kevin E., 1950-
    A concise guide to canon law : a practical handbook for pastoral ministers
    / Kevin E. McKenna.
        p. cm.
    Includes bibliographical references.
    ISBN 0-87793-934-9 (pbk.)
    1. Canon law. 2. Clergy--Handbooks, manuals, etc. I. Title.
LAW
262.9--dc21   99-054585

To Fr. Raymond G. Heisel,

colleague, mentor, and friend

Requiescat in pace

Contents

Baptism   27

Confirmation   37

Marriage 65

Parishes 81

ACKNOWLEDGMENTS

The author is most grateful to Rev. John M. Huels, O.S.M., Very Rev. John A. Renken, Rev. James A. Coriden, and Prof. Michel Thériault, who read various sections of the manuscript and provided corrections and many helpful suggestions. I also owe a debt of gratitude to Cathy Solan, who assisted me in the manuscript production and corrections with her computer skills. Finally, I wish to express my thanks to Bishop Matthew Clark and the staff of the Pastoral Center of the Diocese of Rochester for their continued support and encouragement in this effort.

Preface

Many in today's church question the need for a legal system. Perhaps it is symptomatic of the current climate in the secular world where high profile criminal cases have created great debates about the efficacy and efficiency of justice in the U.S. The church endures today the same scrutiny and questions.

In the church, however, the debate is more basic than how law is administered. Rather, the question is more elemental: Is there a need for a legal system at all? St. Paul, in many of his letters, railed against the legalists within the Jewish community who put observance of the law before the practice of religion: "[We] who know that a person is not justified by works of the law but through faith in Jesus Christ, even we have believed in Christ Jesus that we may be justified by faith in Christ and not by works of the law, because by works of the law no one will be justified" (Gal 2:16).

But at the same time as Paul was giving primacy to faith, he acknowledged a clear role for law: to assist the local churches he had visited to live lives in harmony with the message of Jesus. He had strong practical directives for the many situations facing the early Christian community, including the bringing of lawsuits against pagans (1 Cor 6), eating meats that were offered to idols (1 Cor 8), and the use of various charismatic gifts (1 Cor 14:1-33). One practical procedure concerned the marital relationship of unbelievers with one spouse desirous of baptism (1 Cor 7:12-16), which continues as a part of the church's official marriage law (the "Pauline privilege") even today.

The church today has a need for norms as much as the early church, and for the same reasons. We live as a "people of God," as the Second Vatican Council reminded us. Like any society of people, there are many times when we are jostled and bumped along the road as we make our way through life. Like any society consisting of humans, the members of the church, as we grow to appreciate our rights (as well as our obligations), need to respect the path of our neighbor. Law functions best when it upholds and fosters the dignity of the individual and assures through its directives respect for the dignity of each person.

Those involved in leadership positions within the parish setting today face numerous challenges in their daily ministry. Perhaps most pressing (and at times, confusing and frustrating) is the sacramental life of the church, a core reality of our identity as Catholic Christians. In the years since the Second Vatican Council, there have developed many tensions in the church that have left pastoral leaders in deep quandaries and controversies about what *are* the actual norms of the church as they apply to its sacramental life.

A Concise Guide to Canon Law is an effort to present a compact, usable reference guide in some of the major areas of canon law that affect primarily the pastor, parochial vicar, deacon, and pastoral associate, as well as a variety of pastoral agents now working in the church. More and more parishioners are interested as well in the laws and procedures of the church, especially as they impact their lives as participating members. This book is an effort to distill into a practical format the myriad laws contained in the *Code of Canon Law* with an emphasis on the more practical areas such as the sacraments, declarations of nullity, and consultative bodies.

Each chapter contains a summary of the basic legislation taken from the 1983 *Code of Canon Law* as related to a specific topic. Each summary has been compiled from a variety of canons related to a topic for ease of understanding. References to the canon numbers, should you desire to study the actual canon itself, are found throughout the chapters. Canonical terms that are not explained in the text are printed in **boldface** and can be found in the glossary at the end of the book, along with other commonly used canonical terms and expressions.

In addition, after the summary of the topic, several chapters contain a series of questions and answers, which will hopefully make more practicable the legislation that has been outlined. These include some of the most frequently asked questions that surface in pastoral ministry.

This small book does not claim to be an exhaustive exposition of canon law today. Its scope is much more modest. It is rather intended as an easy-to-use reference guide for pastoral ministers, providing a quick summary in outline form of the major topical areas in canon law (Latin Rite) and thereby answering some pastoral questions that often come up in the day-to-day life of the average pastoral minister. For several reasons, including a diminishing number of ordained clergy, more and more lay people are being given important leadership positions in our Catholic parishes. It seems particularly important that they come grounded with some exposure to this important area of ecclesial life.

Historical Introduction

The legal system that we have in the Catholic Church today is the result of two thousand years of development. Even in the earliest days of the church, it became quite apparent that rules (or norms) would be needed to provide some sense of "belonging" to the group that sought to follow the teachings of Jesus Christ. The Acts of the Apostles recounts a gathering of leaders of the Christian community in Jerusalem to discuss the "gentile" question—how best to assimilate this group into the fellowship of believers (Acts 15). A decision had to be made about how "Jewish" one needed to be in order to be accepted as a disciple of Jesus. This decision—including the provision that circumcision would not be necessary—had long-ranging consequences for the survival of Christianity. It also became clear that an internal structure for decision-making and legislating was needed.

The following is a brief chronological summary of some of the major highlights in the development of the church's legal system:

c. 100 A.D. The *Didache*—a collection of instructions originating in Syria or Palestine pertaining primarily to liturgy and morality. It became the basis for many later collections of laws for the early church. It contained rules about baptism, eucharist, the organization of the Christian community, and the selection and consecration of church officials.

c. 218 The *Traditio Apostolica* of Hippolytus of Rome—a Greek text; a basic compendium of liturgical usages of the church at Rome. It contained rules concerning the consecration of bishops, priests, and deacons as well as regulations for confessors, catechumens, lectors, and other diverse prescriptions concerning life in the community of believers.

c. 250	The *Didascalia Apostolorum*—from either Syria or Palestine, one of the first attempts at assembling a body of **canon law**, touching on many important aspects of community life, including: advice for widows and married couples, fasting, the manner of celebrating eucharist.
c. 300	The *Canones Ecclesiastici Apostolorum*—from either Syria or Egypt, a collection of thirty chapters written in Greek, dealing with both moral norms and disciplinary regulations.
325	Council of Nicaea (the first ecumenical council)—gathering of representatives of the entire church convened for doctrinal and disciplinary consolidation, fixing in place some long-standing practices such as the election of bishops, structural organization (e.g., **dioceses**), and the readmission of schismatics into the church.

The development of **law** was very much linked to the conciliar model of church governance. Bishops gathered in council to discuss important issues of the day that pertained to the life of the church. After coming to some consensus on the issues, norms (or *canons*) were formulated that were later transmitted to other areas where they served as models for local legislation.

Another important early source of law was the decretals (**decrees**) of the popes. By the fourth century, the bishop of Rome was issuing responses to disciplinary inquiries from various bishops. That the pope should be consulted was a logical development, given the increasing prestige of the see of Rome and the availability of **archives** and the presence of legal specialists in Rome who could assist the pope in providing good authoritative answers. These responses soon assumed the status of general law for the entire church.

Late 300s	*Syntagma Canonum*—collection of canons from councils of the church, assembled at Antioch and completed in the fifth century.
c. 500	Dionysius (Dennis) Exiguus' *Liber Decretorum*—a canonical collection by a monk named Dennis, consisting of 50 apostolic canons, 350 canons from various councils of the church, and 38 decrees of various popes. This was a major

collection of laws utilized throughout the church for the next several centuries.

c. 550   *Collectio 50 Titulorum*—collection by an Antiochene lawyer Joannes Scholasticus, who brought together under about fifty titles the law of the church current at that time.

774   *Dionysiana-Hadriana*—collection of laws presented by Pope Adrian I to Charlemagne, a model code based on the *Dionysiana* of Dionysius Exiguus.

c. 800   *Dacheriana*—a French collection of an anonymous priest, of great use during the Carolingian reform, touching on such subjects as penitential discipline and procedural law.

(The following four entries are some individuals who contributed to the development of canon law.)

806-882   Hincmar—archbishop of Rheims, skilled in Roman law and contributor to the science of canon law.

1008-1022   Burchard—bishop of Worms issued his *Decretum*, an effort to reform the clergy of his time and increase the power of the bishops.

1091-1116   Ivo—archbishop of Chartres, fostered reform and respect for papal primacy with his *Tripartita, Decretum*, and *Panormia*.

c. 1140   John Gratian—completed his work, the *Concordantia Discordantium, Canonum* (*A Harmony of Discordant Canons*), or *Decretum*. Up until this time there was great confusion in the area of law due to the vast variety of diffuse collections. Gratian, a monk teaching at the University of Bologna, undertook to harmonize the various collections into a coherent whole, similar to efforts that were currently underway for a comparable **civil law** corpus. His efforts bore fruit in his *Decretum*, which became an enormously important reference work for canonists.

1234	*Decretals of Gregory IX*—collection assembled to include papal decretals and conciliar canons issued since the *Decretum*, assembled by St. Raymond of Peñafort. Since this was formally **promulgated** by the pope it became an authentic collection of laws for the entire church.
1298	*Liber Sextus* (Book Six)—(named thus since it was intended to supplement the five books that made up the *Decretals of Gregory IX*) another collection of laws, this time by Boniface VIII which included his own decretals and those of his predecessors since Gregory IX, as well as the canons of the councils of Lyons (1245 and 1274).
1500	*Corpus Iuris Canonici* (Body of Canon Law)— compilation by John Chappuis and Vitale de Thebis of the major collections of law up until that point, including Gratian's *Decretum*, the *Decretals of Gregory IX*, and other collections. It remained an important source of law for the church up until the promulgation of the first code of canon law (1917).
1545-1563	Council of Trent—attempted to give a canonical as well as a doctrinal basis for the internal reform of the church which included the duties and obligations of clerics, regulations concerning ordinations, criminal proceedings, penitential disciplines, and synods.
1917	*Code of Canon Law*—was an important work of Pope Pius X (1835-1914) in which he attempted to codify the vast canonical tradition into a coherent whole. The actual work was done by a commission of cardinals headed by Cardinal Pietro Gasparri. After consultation with the bishops and major superiors throughout the world, the code was promulgated by Pope Benedict XV, May 27, 1917.

A revision of the *Code of Canon Law* was inaugurated during the pontificate of Pope John XXIII, who announced in 1959 his desire to update the law of the church at the same time he announced an ecumenical council (Vatican II) and a **synod** for the city of Rome. Pope Paul VI determined that the work of the code commission itself would not begin until the conclusion of the Second Vatican Council. The work was finally completed under the pontificate of John Paul II when the *Code* was promulgated, January 25, 1983. In October of 1990, Pope John Paul II was to promulgate the *Code of Canons of the Eastern Churches*, in order that the proper disciplines of the Eastern Churches be maintained and fostered.

Canon Law:
A General Orientation

Like any legal system, **canon law** is a logical, generally coherent, and rational body of rules. The word "canon" is derived from the Greek, *kanon*, referring to a rule or measure. A majority of the canons (or rules of law) are called "ecclesiastical," or "church" laws, since they originate from the church through its leadership and not directly from God ("divine law"). In order to understand its workings, it is important to be familiar with the general principles of canon law that are contained in Book 1 ("General Norms") of the *Code of Canon Law*:

Principle 1: Each *Code* (Latin and Eastern) pertains to its own unique and individual procedures of governance. (c. 1)

The *Code of Canon Law* was **promulgated** by Pope John Paul II in 1983 for the Latin Church. The *Code of Canons of the Eastern Churches* was promulgated in 1990 for the Eastern Churches. Generally speaking, members of the Latin Rite follow the *Code of Canon Law*; members of the Eastern Churches follow the *Code of Canons of the Eastern Churches.*

Principle 2: The canons of the *Code* do not normally address the individual rituals utilized by the church in the celebration of the sacraments. (c. 2)

The manner and detail of ritual celebration of the various sacraments are found in the individual liturgical books that govern each sacrament. For example, the exact ritual for baptism, as well as appropriate instruction regarding the celebration of the sacrament, is found in the *Order of Baptism.* However, some general principles and even some specific norms regarding the celebration of baptism, as well as the other sacraments, can be found in the *Code* (baptism, cc. 849-878).

Principle 3: Laws cannot bind until they are officially promulgated. (cc. 7, 8)

Laws take effect and gain force when the legislator has followed the official procedure for making laws and has made the law known as official legislation. **Ecclesiastical laws** for the entire church become effective as law three months after they have been published in the official commentary of the holy see (see **apostolic see**), the *Acta Apostolicae Sedis* (unless for some special reason another manner of promulgation has been established). **Particular laws** (promulgated by a particular or local church; e.g., **diocese**) take effect one month after they have been promulgated, unless for some reason the law itself contains another date.

Principle 4: Laws are made for the *future* and not for the *past*. (c. 9)

Laws are created to govern circumstances regarding the future. Although past situations may suggest that a law is needed, the law that is then created addresses future circumstances, not the past.

Principle 5: A law must specifically state that it pertains to invalidation to do so. (c. 10)

Some laws within the Code regulate an action or a person who acts in an official capacity and define when such an action is legally effective or when a person can function in a legally effective way. For example, canon 521 §1 states that to assume the office of **pastor** *validly*, one must be a priest. The church could not recognize as pastor a person appointed to that position who was not an ordained presbyter. But since validity (see **valid**) is so important for the proper functioning of the church, the canon must stipulate that importance by reference to validity in the canon itself.

Principle 6: Ecclesiastical laws bind Catholics who have reached the use of reason. (c. 11)

Church laws are made for Catholics, either baptized into the church or received into full union with it. Members of other faith traditions, e.g., Protestants, are not bound by canon law. However, should a member of a Protestant church or another faith tradition (or no religion at all) wish to marry a Roman

Catholic, the marriage is subject to the requirements stipulated in canon law.

Principle 7: **Universal laws** bind every Catholic, regardless of residence; particular laws (made by the proper authority in a particular area, e.g., diocese) bind Catholics in *that* area. (c. 12)

Catholics establish a residence (**domicile**) officially in the church when they have lived in a **parish** (or at least in the diocese) for five years or are residents in the parish (or diocese) and have the intention of remaining there permanently unless called away for some reason.

Sometimes Catholics maintain other residences besides their home which can be referred to as a "**quasi-domicile.**" This can be established by a residence of three months or at least having the intention of remaining there for three months.

Particular laws bind Catholics who have a domicile or a quasi-domicile in the diocesan church where the laws originated and when the person is actually present in that diocese. For example, a local bishop may determine by law that a particular day of the week will be observed as a day of fasting and abstinence in his diocese to promote some work of justice and peace. Catholics in the diocese would not be bound when they are outside of the diocese. Laws normally are considered to apply *territorially* and not *personally*. Transients (people who have no residence and move from place to place) are subject to both universal law and the particular laws of the place in which they are traveling.

Principle 8: It is the creator of the law (legislator) who properly *interprets* the law. (cc. 16-18)

Unlike the tri-partite system of government in the United States with one specific branch, the judicial, interpreting the laws created by the legislative branch, the canonical system invests that authority in the legislator, or in any individual invested by the legislator with that responsibility.

In attempting to understand an ecclesiastical law, one looks to the *text* and to the *context* in which the law appears; if it is still not clear, one makes reference to other similar laws if they should exist, then to the purposes which gave rise to that law, and finally, to the mind of the legislator who created the law.

When a law is created that seeks to establish a *penalty* or *restrict the free exercise of rights* or makes mention of an *exception to the law*, it must be interpreted strictly.

Principle 9: When canon law defers to **civil law** in a particular matter, the civil law has the same effects in canon law. (c. 22)

Sometimes and in some matters, when provision has not been made in canon law, the church accepts the civil law (unless it is contrary to divine law).

Principle 10: The custom of a community is an important developer of law under certain circumstances. (cc. 23-28)

In certain situations, **custom** can create new law. The custom must have been legitimately observed for thirty continuous years by a community that is capable of receiving a law.

Principle 11: In certain circumstances, the appropriate authority can dispense from ecclesiastical laws for a just and reasonable cause. (cc. 85-93)

The church provides for the relaxation of a particular ecclesiastical law by the proper authority when it is clear that such a **dispensation** would contribute to the spiritual good of a person. The bishop can dispense from most universal laws and particular laws of his diocese, with the exception of procedural law, penal law, or those laws for which a dispensation has been reserved to a higher authority (see apostolic see). Many of the marriage **impediments** (pp. 67-71) are of ecclesiastical law and thus can be dispensed by the **local ordinary**.

Sacraments:
General Canonical Principles

The sacraments of the church are the principal means and experiences by which the faith of the church is celebrated and built up. It is the belief of the church that by way of the sacraments and the full participation of the people of God, perfect worship is offered to God through the signs given by Christ. For this reason the church is extremely vigilant that these rites are celebrated with care and reverence and are regulated by proper liturgical norms.

Principle 1: The supervision of the sacramental life of the church is entrusted to the **apostolic see**, whose responsibility includes the determination of the requirements for validity of the sacraments, and also to the **diocesan bishop**, as specified in the law. (c. 838)

Since the sacraments are of central importance to the life of the church, an important effort is made to ensure that the integrity of the sacramental life is preserved. It is the apostolic see which publishes liturgical books and approves vernacular translations of the various rituals that are prepared by the **conferences of bishops** and makes sure that liturgical norms are universally observed. The diocesan bishop issues various norms concerning the liturgical life in his own **diocese** in those areas that have been indicated by the **universal law**.

Principle 2: It is first necessary that one receive baptism before being admitted to the other sacraments. Baptism, confirmation, and eucharist are intimately linked as the sacraments of initiation into the church. (c. 842)

Baptism is understood to be the *gateway* to the other sacraments and to the *life of grace.*

Principle 3: The ministers of the sacraments cannot refuse to administer them to those who are properly disposed, ask for them at an appropriate time, and are not prohibited by the law from receiving them. (c. 843, §1)

Since the sacraments are understood to be necessary for salvation, those entrusted by the church with celebrating the sacraments should take care to make them available when reasonably requested.

Principle 4: Catholic ministers may administer the sacraments to others besides Catholics under certain prescribed conditions. (c. 844)

Catholic ministers may administer the sacraments of penance, eucharist, and anointing of the sick to members of the Oriental Churches not in full communion with the Catholic Church (commonly referred to as the "**Orthodox Churches**") when the members ask for them on their own and are properly disposed. This applies to other churches whom the holy see has judged in a similar condition; e.g., the Polish National Church.

Catholic ministers may also administer these same sacraments to members of other Christian faith traditions when it is a case of danger of death or a grave necessity that has been determined in norms issued by the local diocesan bishop or the **conference of bishops**. Those seeking the sacraments in the Catholic Church must ask for them on their own and not be able to receive the sacrament from their own minister. They must also manifest the same faith in the sacrament and be properly disposed.

Principle 5: No sacred minister on his own may change or alter the liturgical books that have been approved by the holy see. (c. 846)

Principle 6: Those who administer the sacraments may not demand any payment or offering beyond what has been approved by the appropriate authority. (c. 848)

No one must ever be deprived of receiving the sacraments because of an inability to make an offering.

Baptism

The sacrament of baptism is the first sacrament received and the gateway to the other sacraments of the church. Through the reception of this sacrament, individuals are freed from sin and reborn in the new life of grace; there is also a configuration to Christ with the imparting of an indelible character and incorporation into the community of the faithful, the church.

Baptism Ritual (c. 850)

The *Ritual for Baptism* should be consulted for the rite that is followed for the celebration of the sacrament. In urgent necessity, all that is required is the pouring of water and the formula: "I baptize you in the name of the Father and of the Son and of the Holy Spirit."

Adult Baptism (c. 851, 1°)

Adults who wish to be baptized are enrolled into the **catechumenate**. Unless a grave reason prevents it, the adult who is baptized receives immediately afterward the sacraments of confirmation and eucharist.

Infant Baptism (c. 851, 2°)

For the baptism of infants (children who have not obtained the **age of reason**, considered to be the age of seven), the parents and, secondarily, the sponsor(s) have responsibility for sharing their own faith through this sacrament. The **pastor** is to make sure that the parents are well prepared through an appropriate catechesis about their important role in the spiritual formation of the child.

Day and Place for Baptism (cc. 856, 857, 860)

The actual celebration of baptism should take place on a Sunday or, if possible, at the Easter Vigil, in the **parish** church of the person to be baptized (or, in the case of an infant, the parents' parish). Only for a grave cause and by permission of the **ordinary** may a baptism be celebrated in a private home. It is celebrated either by immersion or by the pouring of water.

Ordinary Minister (c. 861)

The ordinary minister of this sacrament is a bishop, priest, or deacon. If the ordinary minister is impeded, a catechist or other person deputed to this task by the **local ordinary**, as well as any person with the correct intention in case of necessity, may baptize.

Requirements for Baptism (cc. 865, 867, 868)

In order to be baptized, an adult must have freely manifested his or her desire to receive the sacrament, been properly prepared and instructed for it, and participated in the catechumenate. They should also express sorrow for any sins they have committed.

In case of danger of death, it is sufficient that the person have some knowledge of the Christian truths and express some sign of their desire to receive the sacrament and promises to observe the commandments of the Christian religion.

Parents should see to it that their infants are baptized within the first weeks of their birth. In danger of death, the infant should be baptized immediately. At least one of the parents (or guardian) of an infant to be baptized must agree to the baptism; in danger of death, the baptism is to be celebrated even if one or both parents object. There must be a founded hope that the child will be raised in the Catholic faith. If such hope is lacking, the baptism may be delayed in accordance with **particular law**, with an explanation for such a delay communicated to the parents.

Doubtful Baptism (c. 869)

In situations where there exists a doubt as to whether or not baptism has been conferred, and the doubt remains after serious investigation, baptism should be conferred conditionally, i.e., "If you have not been baptized, I baptize you. . . ."A person who has been baptized into another Christian faith tradition should *not* be conditionally baptized unless after serious investigation of the ritual used and the intention of the minister conferring the sacrament there remain doubts as to the validity of the baptism received. If conditional baptism is then required, the doctrine of the sacrament is to be explained and the reasons provided (to the parents, if an infant).

Baptismal Sponsors (cc. 872-874)

A sponsor assists an adult to be baptized, or assists the parents in presenting an infant for baptism. The sponsor assists the newly baptized in living the Christian life. If two sponsors are chosen, they are to be of different sexes.

The qualifications for serving as a sponsor are:

1. designated for this role by the one to be baptized (or by the parents in the case of an infant);

2. 16 years of age or older (the local bishop may establish a different age; the minister of baptism may also make an exception in a particular case);

3. a Catholic, confirmed and who has received the eucharist, leading a life in conformity with the faith and the role assumed as a sponsor;

4. not bound by any **canonical penalty**;

5. not a parent of the one to be baptized.

A baptized person who is not Catholic may serve as a witness to the baptism with a Catholic sponsor.

Proving Baptism (c. 876)

To prove the conferral of baptism, it is sufficient to obtain the declaration of a single witness or even the oath of the baptized person if the person was baptized as an adult.

Recording Baptism (c. 877)

The pastor of the place where the baptism is celebrated is to record the baptism immediately in the baptismal register, including the name of the baptized, minister, parents, sponsor(s) (and witness), place and date of conferred baptism, and place and date of birth. If the child's mother is not married, her name is included in the register if there is public proof of maternity or if the mother asks willingly in writing or before two witnesses that this be done; in the case of the father, his name is to be inserted if his paternity is established either by public proof or by his declaration before the pastor and two witnesses. Otherwise, the names of the father and or mother are not indicated.

If a child is adopted, the names of the adopting parents are recorded; the names of the natural parents are also included in accordance with local **civil law** and the prescriptions of the **conference of bishops**.

Membership in a Ritual Church (cc. 111-112)

Within the Catholic Church, there exists the Latin Church and twenty-one autonomous Eastern Churches with their own hierarchy, in communion with the Bishop of Rome.

A person obtains membership in a **ritual church** through baptism or transfer.

Baptism Into a Ritual Church (c. 111)

A child born of parents who belong to the Latin Church is ascribed to the Latin Church when baptized. If one parent is not a member of the Latin Church, but both parents *agree* to have the child baptized in the Latin Church, the child is ascribed to it by baptism. If there is no agreement between the parents, the child becomes a member of the ritual church of the father. Anyone to be baptized who is fourteen years of age or older may choose the ritual church in which they wish to be baptized.

Ritual Church Transfer (c. 112)

One may transfer from one ritual church to another by obtaining permission from the holy see (see **apostolic see**). Should a member of the Latin Church wish to transfer to an Eastern Church that has a bishop with jurisdiction in the same **diocese**, the agreement of both bishops is sufficient for the transfer and no intervention of the holy see is required.

A spouse at the time of marriage or during marriage can declare a transferal from their ritual church to that of their spouse; they may then return to their original ritual church when the marriage has ended.

Children under fourteen years of age, when a parent has transferred to the ritual church of the other spouse, likewise are transferred to the common ritual church. Similarly, children of parents in a mixed marriage, when the Catholic parent transfers to another ritual church, likewise transfer to the new ritual church. However, when such children reach fourteen years of age, they may return to their original ritual church.

The custom of receiving the sacraments according to the rite of another ritual church does not carry with it the enrollment into that church.

In accordance with the Vatican II **decree** *Orientalium Ecclesiarum* (no. 4), baptized non-Catholics coming into full communion with the Catholic Church must enter the Catholic Church through the ritual church most similar to their own; e.g., Protestants come into full union with the Catholic Church through the Latin Church, Greek Orthodox through the Greek Catholic Church, etc. Any exception must receive the permission of the holy see or the two bishops who share jurisdiction.

1. *May a pastoral minister refuse baptism to a child of parents who are not practicing Catholics?*

Unfortunately, it frequently happens that one or both parents presenting a child to the church for baptism do not practice their faith. A variety of reasons may be present. A once active faith for one reason or another may have grown dormant. One parent may have had a "bad experience" with a pastoral minister, perhaps several years ago, and now feels estranged from the church. There may be a serious crisis of faith. Or, perhaps through sheer laziness, one or both parents have developed new priorities that do not include the church.

This can present a delicate and awkward challenge to the pastoral minister, conscious that the ceremony for infant baptism is directed to the parents and godparents and their commitment to share their own faith life with the child. Canon 868, §1, 2° requires a "founded hope" that the infant will be brought up in the Catholic religion, before the sacrament is administered. If such hope is altogether lacking, the baptism is to be delayed and the parents informed of this decision. Each diocese should develop its own policies concerning the deferral of the sacrament. Pastoral experience over the years would indicate that an outright refusal of the sacrament rarely results in a return to the church. In fact, it may permanently estrange the parents from the practice of their faith. More frequently, patient and persistent sessions conducted by the pastoral minister with the parents, where the connection is made between the meaning of the sacrament, the faith life of the child, and the parents' faith life can lead to an appreciation of the parents' important role and ultimately to a "well-founded" hope being established.

2. *May a permanent deacon be the ordinary minister for baptism?*

For many Catholics there is an automatic identification of the sacrament of baptism with the priest. However, in accordance with c. 861, §1, the ordinary minister of the sacrament of baptism is a bishop, priest, or deacon. Thus, a permanent deacon would be an ordinary minister of the sacrament.

3. *May a pastor refuse to admit a person to the RCIA program?*

The *Rite of Christian Initiation of Adults* is a process by which unbaptized adults seeking entrance into the Catholic Church participate in several rites, experience opportunities for prayer, and learn more about the gospel message of Jesus and the church. It is designed for those who "after hearing the mystery of Christ proclaimed, consciously and freely seek the living God and enter the way of faith and conversion as the Holy Spirit opens their hearts" (*RCIA*, #1). Therefore it would not seem appropriate for a pastor to deny someone the opportunity to begin this path of discernment. However, it is possible that a person who has been baptized into a separated ecclesial community, e.g., Methodist, Lutheran, etc., may desire to participate in the RCIA program. In such situations, the *Reception of Baptized Christians Into the Full Communion of the Catholic Church* would be the appropriate liturgical rite. These persons are referred to as candidates and have a distinct status, by virtue of their baptism, and need a distinct catechesis in preparation for their reception into the church. A pastor therefore would correctly direct such an inquirer into a separate program.

4. *May a person in an invalid marriage be admitted to the RCIA program?*

A person who is in a marriage which the church cannot recognize as **valid** due to the presence of an **impediment** such as a prior bond is still eligible for admittance into the RCIA program. However, before receiving baptism, it would be necessary that the catechumen's marriage situation be resolved (e.g., obtaining a declaration of nullity) so that the person be properly disposed and able to celebrate the sacraments of initiation. It is therefore most important that parish staff interview potential catechumens before they proceed too far into the program so that the person with an invalid marriage is aware of this potential difficulty and so the staff may assist the catechumen in whatever canonical procedures may be necessary before the person is initiated into the church. Since people enter this process at different stages of their faith journey, it is appropriate that there be flexibility for scheduling the time for the actual celebration of the Rites for Christian Initiation for each individual, rather than assuming all participants will pass through this process at the same time.

5. *May a minor be admitted to an RCIA program against the wishes of his or her parents?*

In **canon law**, a person who is under eighteen years of age is considered a minor. Canon 98, §2 states that a minor remains subject to the authority of parents in the exercise of his or her rights. However, this same canon goes on to state an exception—areas in which minors are exempt by divine or canon law. By divine law, all are impelled to seek the truth of faith and salvation. So even if a parent objects to the enrollment of their child in an RCIA program, a minor could still be admitted. Practically, however, one would question the wisdom of such an admission, given the lack of support the minor would have in the practice of the faith from the parents.

6. *May someone in an invalid marriage serve as a sponsor for the RCIA program?*

A sponsor is that person who accompanies a candidate who is seeking admission as a catechumen into the church. The qualification for this role is somewhat limited: he or she must be able to stand as a witness to the

A Concise Guide to Canon Law

candidate's moral character, faith, and intention (*RCIA*, #10). It is quite possible, and the *Rite* itself states, that another person may serve later in the role of godparent for the same catechumen. Although not strictly prohibited, it would seem incongruous for persons to serve as sponsors and be called on to testify to the fitness of a candidate for acceptance as a catechumen if they themselves are in an irregular situation in their relationship to the church.

7. *When a child has been adopted and previously baptized, under which parents' names is the baptism recorded?*

In accordance with c. 877, §3 in the case of an adopted child, the names of the adopting parents are recorded in the baptismal register and, if at least the natural parents' names are recorded in the civil records of the particular region, their names are also included. The National Conference of Catholic Bishops has proposed as a complementary norm that for children baptized after their adoption is finalized, a simple notation is included in the baptismal register that the child is adopted. The fact that the child is adopted is not furnished on an issued baptismal certificate. In the case of a child baptized before the adoption is finalized, and in accordance with the civil law of the jurisdiction, the names of the natural parents (in parentheses), the names of the adoptive parents, the child's former surname (in parentheses), and the new surname, along with a notation that the child was adopted, are all included in the baptismal register. When a baptismal certificate is issued for this latter case, it would contain only the names of the adoptive parents and the child's new legal surname, along with the information concerning date and place of baptism and the name of the minister of the sacrament. The names of the sponsors are not given. After the adoption is finalized, a baptismal entry can be made in the baptismal register of the adoptive parents' parish citing the date and location of the original baptismal record, and providing only the names of the adoptive parents, and the place and date of birth. Parish personnel with access to baptismal registers may not disclose in any way that a person was adopted.

8. *May a non-Catholic serve as a baptismal sponsor?*

To serve in the role of sponsor it is required that the person be a Catholic, who has been confirmed and received eucharist, leading a life in harmony with the faith and role to be undertaken (c. 874, §1, 3°). However, in accordance with c. 874, §2, a non-Catholic baptized person may serve as a *witness*. This person could testify at a later time to the fact that the baptism was indeed celebrated. They must serve in this capacity with a Catholic sponsor.

Confirmation

The sacrament of confirmation imparts a character and enables the person who has been baptized to continue on the journey of initiation into the Christian faith, by the grace of the Holy Spirit. Those who receive this sacrament are empowered to witness to Christ in word and in deed, and to proclaim the gospel message.

Conferral of Sacrament (c. 880)

The essential elements of the sacrament are the anointing on the forehead with **chrism**, which is done by the imposition of hands, and through the words that are given in the ritual for the sacrament.

The sacred oil that is used, holy chrism, must be consecrated by a bishop—even if a presbyter is celebrating the sacrament.

Ordinary Minister of Sacrament (cc. 882-888)

The ordinary minister of the sacrament in the Latin Rite is a bishop. Priests may also administer confirmation:

✛ When the priest, who by virtue of his office (or after being given a mandate by the bishop), baptizes someone who is no longer an infant or receives someone into full union with the Catholic Church, he also confirms.

✛ When there is danger of death, a **pastor** or any priest should confirm someone who has not received this sacrament.

✛ In case of necessity, the **diocesan bishop** may grant the faculty to one or more specified priests.

✛ For a grave cause, the bishop or a priest with the faculty to confirm may associate other priests with him to confer the sacrament.

Eligibility for the Sacrament (cc. 889-891)

All persons who have been baptized are capable of receiving the sacrament of confirmation. The sacrament is usually conferred at the **age of reason** (unless the **conference of bishops** determines another age, or in danger of death, or the minister of the sacrament determines that a grave reason suggests otherwise). Pastors and others concerned with the celebration of the sacrament should make sure that an appropriate catechesis is provided for candidates.

Confirmation Sponsor (cc. 892-893)

A sponsor (ideally the same sponsor for baptism) assists the person to be confirmed by joining the candidate in his or her journey of faith, before and after the celebration of the sacrament, helping the candidate to live as a true witness to Jesus Christ. To be a sponsor, one must have the qualifications for a baptismal sponsor (see p. 29).

Registration of Sacrament (cc. 894-896)

After the sacrament has been celebrated, the names of the confirmed, the minister, the parents and sponsors, and the place and date of the celebration of the sacrament is to be noted in a confirmation register maintained by the diocesan **curia**; however, the conference of bishops or the diocesan bishop may determine that such a register is to be maintained by parishes in the **diocese**. The pastor is to notify the church of baptism that confirmation has been celebrated, so that this may be recorded as a notation in the appropriate baptismal register.

1. *May a parent serve as a confirmation sponsor?*

The requirements for serving as a confirmation sponsor are the same as those of a baptismal sponsor. In fact, it is strongly encouraged that the baptismal sponsor serve in the same capacity for confirmation. Two separate roles are envisioned for the parents and sponsors at baptism. The parents publicly ask that the child be baptized and accept the responsibility to enable the child to know God, to receive confirmation, and to participate in the holy eucharist. The godparents accept the responsibility of helping the parents in their most important role of raising the child in the Catholic faith. Canon 874, §1, 5° states that the role of a sponsor may not be assumed by a parent of the child to be baptized.

2. *At what age have the bishops in the U.S. determined confirmation is to be celebrated?*

Canon 891 states that the sacrament of confirmation is to be conferred on the faithful at about the age of discretion (usually around the age of seven) unless the conference of bishops determines another age or there is danger of death or if in the judgment of the minister a grave cause urges otherwise. In the United States, the National Conference of Catholic Bishops, by **decree** of July 1, 1994, has established that confirmation is to be celebrated between the age of discretion and eighteen years of age. The exceptions mentioned in c. 891 (danger of death and grave cause as judged by the minister of the sacrament) must also be kept in mind. The local bishop is free to determine certain specifications in his own diocese (e.g., catechesis in preparation for the sacrament) but may not establish a specific age which would be contrary to the age range confirmed in the N.C.C.B. decree by the holy see in 1994.

3. *May a pastor who baptizes a child of ten years of age delay confirmation to a later time so that the child participates in a separate confirmation program?*

A child of ten has reached the age of reason (usually around the age of seven) and is of "catechetical age." *The Rite of Christian Initiation for Children Who Have Reached Catechetical Age* states that such children are capable of "receiving and nurturing a personal faith and of recognizing an obligation of conscience" (*RCIC,* #252). For purposes of Christian initiation, children who have reached the age of reason are considered to be adults (c. 852, §1). Thus, their formation should follow the same pattern as that of adults, appropriately modified for their age, and they should receive the sacraments of baptism, confirmation, and eucharist at the Easter Vigil (see *National Statutes for the Catechumenate,* #18).

4. *May a priest (instead of a bishop) ever administer the sacrament of confirmation?*

The diocesan bishop is the ordinary minister of confirmation in the Latin Rite (c. 882). It is the responsibility of the diocesan bishop to administer confirmation personally or to see to it that the sacrament is administered by another bishop (c. 884, §1). There are also opportunities provided in the code when a presbyter may confirm. Canon 883, 2° addresses the situation when a presbyter with an office (e.g., pastor) or with a specific mandate from the diocesan bishop baptizes someone who is no longer an infant or receives a person who is already baptized seeking admission into full union with the Catholic Church. By law presbyters in this situation validly confirm so that the sacraments of initiation (baptism, confirmation, eucharist) may be celebrated together. In danger of death, the pastor or any presbyter may by law confirm (c. 883, 3°). Also, in case of necessity, the diocesan bishop may give the faculty to confirm to one or more specified presbyters (c. 884, §1). Presbyters who are assisting at a confirmation with a bishop, or even with a presbyter who by law or special concession is confirming, may be enlisted to administer the sacrament at that celebration.

Eucharist

The eucharist is the summit of all Catholic worship and life, the memorial of the death and resurrection of the Lord. All the other sacraments lead to the eucharist.

Presider at Eucharist (c. 900)

Only a validly ordained priest may preside at the celebration of the eucharist. Priests are strongly encouraged to celebrate Mass frequently, even daily. They are not to celebrate the eucharist more than once a day except for those occasions when the law permits (e.g., Christmas, All Souls Day), or when due to a lack of priests, the **ordinary**, for a just cause, permits the priest to celebrate twice or even three times in one day on Sundays or holydays of obligation.

Concelebration With Ministers of Other Churches (c. 908)

Priests may not concelebrate the eucharist with ministers of churches (or ecclesial communities) not in full communion with the Catholic Church.

Distribution of Holy Communion (c. 910)

The ordinary minister for the distribution of holy communion is a bishop, priest, or deacon. Acolytes or other members of the faithful deputed for this function serve as extraordinary ministers.

Admittance to Eucharist (cc. 912-914)

Any baptized person whom the law does not prohibit may be admitted to the eucharist. For children, it is required that they have been properly prepared and have sufficient knowledge (e.g., can distinguish the Body of Christ from ordinary food). Parents and **pastors** have primary responsibility for seeing to it that children who have reached the **age of reason** receive proper catechesis for the reception of first communion, preceded by sacramental confession.

Proper Reception of Eucharist (cc. 916, 919, 920)

A person conscious of grave sin may not receive communion without prior sacramental confession unless for a grave reason the person is unable to celebrate reconciliation, in which case a perfect act of contrition is made with a firm intention to confess as soon as possible.

One who is to receive eucharist is to abstain from food or drink (with the exception of water and medicines) for at least one hour before receiving communion. The priest who celebrates two or three times in one day may take nourishment between Masses even if an hour doesn't intervene; also, the elderly or infirm and those who take care of them may receive communion without fasting.

All the faithful must receive eucharist at least once a year. This should be fulfilled during the Easter season, unless it is fulfilled, for a just cause, at some other time during the year.

Eucharistic Celebration (cc. 924-926, 932, 938)

The Mass is to be celebrated with recently made unleavened bread and natural wine of the grape. Communion may be distributed under both forms in compliance with liturgical norms. It is never permitted to consecrate one matter without the other (e.g., just the bread or just the wine) or both elements outside the eucharist. In celebrating and distributing the eucharist, clerics are to wear the prescribed liturgical vestments. The Mass is to be celebrated upon a dedicated or blessed altar. The eucharist should be celebrated in a sacred place unless necessity would demand another appropriate place, which must be a respectable location. In this case, at least a table should be utilized with corporal and cloth. The eucharist is to be reserved regularly in one tabernacle in a church or **oratory**. The tabernacle is to be unmovable, solid, opaque, and locked.

✛ Priests are permitted to accept an offering to apply the Mass for a definite intention when celebrating or concelebrating Mass.

✛ Any appearance of trafficking or commerce in regards to Mass offerings is to be strictly avoided.

✛ Separate Masses are to be celebrated for individual intentions that have been accepted. If a sum of money is contributed without any mention of the number of Masses requested, the number is computed according to the local offering in use in that area.

✛ A priest may accept only one offering each day for Masses celebrated, with the exception of Christmas. Any additional offerings must be given to the purposes proposed by the ordinary. The provincial council (see **province**) of an area determines the offering for the entire province. No priest may request more than the prescribed offering. Lacking such a provincial determination, it is up to the ordinary to make such a determination.

✛ It is not permitted for a priest to accept more Mass offerings to be applied for himself than can be celebrated within a year. The pastor is to retain a book that records Mass intentions accepted and stipends given and the date of celebration. This book is examined by the ordinary (or a delegate) annually.

1. *May the eucharist ever be refused to a communicant?*

   According to c. 843, §1, sacred ministers cannot refuse the sacraments to those who ask for them at appropriate times, are properly disposed, and are not prohibited from receiving them. In fact, c. 912 declares that any baptized person who is not prohibited by law may and must be admitted to holy communion. In addition, c. 213 speaks of the right of the faithful to receive the spiritual goods of the church, especially the word of God and the sacraments. However, c. 915 states that those who are excommunicated or interdicted after the imposition or declaration of the penalty or obstinately persist in grave sin are not to be admitted to the eucharist. The *Code* does not overly restrict access to the eucharist. When admission to the eucharist must be restricted, the law would insist that very serious reasons be present, since such exclusion would be denying a fundamental right.

2. *May the mentally handicapped receive the eucharist?*

   Canon 912 states that any baptized person who is not prohibited by law can and must be admitted to the eucharist. In addition, c. 913, §1 says that for the administration of holy communion to children in the Latin Rite, it is required that they have sufficient knowledge and careful preparation so as to understand the mystery of Christ according to their capacity, and that they be able to receive the Body of the Lord with faith and devotion. It is usually presumed that at the age of reason (about seven) the child should be able to make some basic distinctions about the difference of the eucharist from ordinary food. There are no precise guidelines provided in the *Code* concerning the distribution of eucharist to the mentally handicapped, but analogously to the requirements for those making first eucharist, the person should have some understanding of the "specialness" of the eucharist from ordinary food. This knowledge may come from observing others with reverence receiving holy communion. If there is no **particular law** in this matter, then in accordance with c. 912, pastors should be vigilant in protecting the right of the baptized to be admitted to eucharist.

3. *How many times in one day may someone receive the eucharist?*

Canon 917 states that a person who has received the eucharist may receive it again on the same day only during the celebration of the eucharist itself. A question was raised about the interpretation of this canon shortly after the promulgation of the new Code. Was the canon suggesting that a person could receive eucharist several times a day, as long as it was received in the context of Mass? Or was the Latin word for "again" (*iterum*) to be translated really as "a second time"? The Pontifical Commission for the Authentic Interpretation of the Code of Canon Law in 1984 ruled that *iterum* should be interpreted as "a second time"—that a person who has received eucharist should receive it only a second time in one day.

4. *May a non-Catholic ever receive eucharist at a Catholic Mass?*

Catholic ministers may distribute the sacraments of penance, eucharist, and anointing of the sick to those who are members of the Oriental Churches which do not have full communion with the Catholic Church (commonly referred to as "**Orthodox Churches**") when they ask for these sacraments on their own and are properly disposed to receive the sacraments (see c. 844, §3). This would also be applicable to members of other churches which are in the same condition as the Oriental Churches as far as the sacraments are concerned (e.g., the Polish National Church). Catholic ministers may administer these same sacraments to other Christians when a person is in danger of death or for another grave reason, in the judgment of the **diocesan bishop** or the **conference of bishops**. The requirements are that these individuals are in a situation where they are unable to approach a minister of their own community, ask for the sacrament on their own, and manifest Catholic faith in these sacraments, while being properly disposed (see c. 844, §4).

5. *May a host with gluten removed be used in communion for a person who is unable to tolerate gluten in wheat flour?*

"Gluten" is the substance found in wheat bread that gives cohesiveness to the dough. Many people, especially those suffering from celiac disease, have a low tolerance for gluten and cannot receive the hosts used in most **parishes** for eucharist. On June 19, 1995, the Congregation for the Doctrine of the Faith issued a letter to the heads of Episcopal Conferences that dealt with the use of "low-gluten" altar breads. The Congregation in its letter stated that low-gluten altar bread is valid matter provided the hosts "contain the amount of gluten sufficient to obtain the confection of bread, that there is no addition of foreign materials, and that the procedure for making such hosts is not such as to alter the nature of the substance of bread." Without the gluten the substance could not be identified as bread, and therefore would be considered invalid matter for eucharist. If a communicant would be unable to consume the smallest particle of gluten, he or she should receive under the form of wine only.

6. *When may a communion service instead of Mass be properly celebrated?*

Canon 1248, §2 makes reference to those situations on a Sunday or holyday of obligation when participation in the eucharist is impossible because a priest is lacking or for some other grave reason. The canon recommends that the faithful take part in the liturgy of the word in the parish church or in another sacred place, according to the prescriptions of the diocesan bishop. Another option presented is to engage in prayer as a family or perhaps with a group of families. In June of 1988 the Congregation for Divine Worship issued a *Directory* for "Sunday Celebrations in the Absence of a Priest." This was an attempt to respond to requests from various **conferences of bishops** who were seeking some structured service for the increasingly common situation when priests were not available in certain regions and areas for Mass. This document stressed that alternatives to Mass should take place only when real circumstances require the decision to have Sunday celebrations in the absence of a priest. The first thing to be ascertained is whether the faithful can go to a nearby church to participate in the eucharistic mystery (#18). Among the forms of celebration found in liturgical tradition when Mass is not possible is the celebration of the word of God and also, its completion, when possible, by eucharistic communion (#20). Another recommendation is the possibility of celebrating the liturgy of the hours (e.g., morning prayer), which could also be followed by communion (#33). It is the responsibility of the diocesan bishop to determine, after hearing the **presbyteral council**, whether Sunday assemblies without the celebration of Mass should be held on a regular basis in the **diocese** (#24).

Penance

The sacrament of penance is the sacrament in which the faithful, acknowledging sorrow for sins committed after baptism and with the desire to reform their lives, obtain forgiveness from God by confession of sins to a priest. By means of this sacrament, those who confess their sins are reconciled to the church for their offenses.

Individual Confession (c. 960)

Individual and integral confession of sins and absolution are the only ordinary way by which a member of the church, aware of serious sin, is reconciled with God and the church. Only physical or moral impossibility excuses a person from such confession; reconciliation can then take place by another means.

General Absolution (cc. 961-963)

General absolution—when absolution is granted by a priest without private individual confession of sins—can be imparted when:

✤ there is imminent danger of death and there is no time for the priest to hear the confession of the individual or individuals;

✤ a large number of penitents has assembled and the number of confessors available would be *inadequate* for what would be time to suitably hear the confessions and not deprive the penitents of sacramental grace or holy communion for a long time.

The **diocesan bishop** judges if the conditions for the imparting of general absolution are present, and he may determine general cases when general absolution can be utilized in his **diocese** with criteria that are provided by the **conference of bishops**.

For a person to validly receive general absolution it is necessary that the person be suitably disposed and also intend to confess individually in due time any serious sins. When feasible, this should be explained to all those participating in general absolution. A person who receives general absolution with serious sin is to confess individually before receiving another general absolution, unless for a just cause this is not possible.

Minister of the Sacrament (cc. 965, 967, 976, 983)

Only a priest is the minister of the sacrament of reconciliation. Priests who receive the faculty to hear confessions in their own diocese may legitimately hear confessions everywhere unless a **local ordinary** denies it in a particular case. When a local ordinary **revokes** the faculty of a priest to hear confessions he is to inform the **ordinary** of the cleric's diocese of **incardination** or competent superior, if a religious.

Even if he lacks the faculty to hear confessions, any priest validly and licitly hears the confession and absolves from any sins and censures one in danger of death.

The **seal of confession** is inviolable; it is a crime for a priest to in any way betray the penitent by word or in any other manner for any reason.

Obligation to Confess (cc. 988, 989)

The faithful are obliged to confess any serious sins at least once a year. They must confess in kind and number all serious sins committed after baptism that have not previously been confessed in individual confession.

1. *When may general absolution (form no. 3) be used for the celebration of reconciliation?*

   The 1983 *Code* states in c. 960 that "individual and integral confession and absolution constitute the only ordinary way by which the faithful person who is aware of serious sin is reconciled with God and with the Church. . . ." There are also two other rites provided by the church in the revised *Penance Rite* of 1973. In addition to the *Rite of Reconciliation of Individual Penitents* there is also a *Rite of Reconciliation of Several Penitents With Individual Confession* and *Absolution* and a *Rite for Reconciliation of Several Penitents With General Confession and Absolution*. This last rite of reconciliation states in the ritual's introduction the occasions when use of the rite is considered lawful: in addition to cases involving danger of death, it may also be utilized when there is a grave need. This is explained as a situation when in view of the number of penitents, sufficient confessors are not available to hear individual confessions properly within a suitable period of time, so that the penitents would have to go, through no fault of their own, without sacramental grace or holy communion for a long time. This may not be used, as the introduction states, for the sole reason of the large number of penitents, as may be the case on the occasion of some major feast or pilgrimage (see *Rite of Penance*, #31). Canon 961 clarifies that the judgment and decision about the presence of such circumstances are reserved to the diocesan bishop, in light of criteria that have been developed by the episcopal conference (#32).

2. *May a child receive first eucharist before receiving first penance?*

   Canon 914, in describing the responsibility of parents and **pastors** for the preparation for first eucharist, also states that this celebration should be preceded by sacramental confession. For several years, experimentation was permitted by the holy see in an effort to study the possibility of a later reception of first penance which would recognize the growing development of conscience in the child and possibly a better appreciation of the sacrament by an older child (e.g., third or fourth grade). The order of celebration is now penance to precede first eucharist. It is also important to remember that in accordance with the Council of Trent, only those conscious of serious sin must confess before receiving eucharist, which is applicable to those receiving first eucharist. All candidates for first eucharist should be properly prepared and catechized concerning the sacrament of penance.

Anointing of the Sick

The sacrament of the anointing of the sick is the celebration of the healing power of the risen Lord, in which Christ's faithful who are seriously ill are anointed with oil by a priest, who follows the rites as prescribed in the proper liturgical book.

Sacred Oil (c. 999)

The oil that is used in the anointing of the sick is blessed by the bishop or one equivalent in law to a **diocesan bishop**. Any priest, in case of necessity, may bless the oil, but only in the actual celebration of the sacrament.

Sacred Anointing (c. 1000)

In celebrating the sacrament of the anointing of the sick, the priest should carefully follow the ritual and anoint the palms of the hand and forehead as prescribed. However, *in case of necessity*, one anointing is permitted on the forehead, or any part of the body, while saying the entire formula. For a serious reason, the priest may also utilize an instrument instead of anointing with his own hand.

Opportunities for Celebration (cc. 1001, 1002)

Pastors and those close to the sick should remain vigilant to the needs of the sick and make sure that an opportunity is provided for this sacrament. This sacrament can also be celebrated communally, gathering the sick in one location and following the celebration as prescribed in the liturgical books and the directives provided by the diocesan bishop.

Minister of the Sacrament (c. 1003)

Only a priest may administer the sacrament of the anointing of the sick. Pastors and those charged with pastoral care of souls have the duty and right to administer the sacrament to those entrusted to their care. Any other priest, however, may administer the sacrament with at least the presumed permission of the aforementioned priest.

Eligibility to Receive Sacrament (cc. 1004-1006)

Those eligible for the sacrament include those who are in *danger* due to sickness or old age. The sacrament can be repeated whenever the person again falls into serious illness or even if after convalescence becomes seriously ill again, or in the course of their illness enters a more serious crisis. The sacrament may be celebrated even if there is doubt as to whether the person has reached the **age of reason**, whether the person is seriously ill, or whether the person is dead. The anointing can be conferred upon a person who would have requested it when they were in control of their faculties.

1. *How many times may a person receive the anointing of the sick in the course of the same illness?*

   In the sacrament of the anointing of the sick the church commends to the suffering and glorified Lord those faithful who are dangerously sick so that he relieve and save them (see c. 998). This sacrament can be administered to members of the faithful who have reached the use of reason. The sacrament can be administered whenever after convalescence the person falls ill again or whenever a more serious crisis develops during the same sickness (c. 1004, §2).

2. *May a deacon administer the sacrament of the anointing of the sick?*

   Every priest, and only a priest, validly administers the anointing of the sick (c. 1003, §1). This question concerning the feasibility of deacons administering this sacrament has been posed on numerous occasions to the holy see, which has yet to change the current discipline.

3. *Can the anointing of the sick be administered to someone who has died?*

   The sacrament is to be administered when there is a doubt whether the sick person has attained the use of reason, whether the person is dangerously ill, or whether the person is dead (c. 1005).

Sacred Orders

The sacrament of ordination celebrates the consecration and deputation to sacred ministry for service to the people of God of certain members of the Christian community. There are three orders of sacred ministry: the episcopacy, the presbyterate, and the diaconate. This sacrament is conferred by the imposition of hands and the prayer of consecration by a bishop, as found in the liturgical books for the particular grade of order.

Minister of the Sacrament (cc. 1012, 1015, 1016)

Candidates for ordination to the **presbyterate** or to the **diaconate** are ordained by their own bishop or by another bishop, providing **dimissorial letters** have been supplied, which attest to the eligibility of the candidate for ordination. The proper bishop for ordination of a candidate to the diaconate is the bishop of the **diocese** where the candidate has a **domicile**, or where he will commit himself to service. The proper bishop of a candidate for the presbyterate of the secular clergy is the bishop where the candidate has been incardinated (see **incardination**).

Eligibility for the Sacrament (cc. 1024, 1025)

Only a baptized male may validly receive the sacrament of holy orders. In addition, candidates for ordination to the diaconate or presbyterate must:

✛ have completed a period of probation;

✛ have the required qualities as judged by his proper bishop or religious superior;

✛ not have any **irregularities** or impediments to receive orders;

✛ have received the sacrament of confirmation;

+ have submitted to their bishop or proper superior a letter in their own hand, petitioning for the order;

+ have been received and accepted by the bishop or proper superior in a rite of candidacy;

+ have received the ministries of acolyte and lector;

+ have submitted a signed declaration in their own hand testifying to their own personal freedom in receiving sacred orders, and that they will perpetually devote themselves to the ministry;

+ if an unmarried candidate for diaconate and candidates for the presbyterate, in a prescribed rite assume publicly the obligation of celibacy (or have professed perpetual vows in a **religious institute**).

All who are to be ordained to any grade of sacred orders are to make a retreat of at least five days in a place and manner determined by the **ordinary**.

Requirements for Ordination to Diaconate and Presbyterate (cc. 1026-1032)

In order for one to be ordained, he ought to possess:

+ freedom from any coercion in receiving orders;

+ an accurate formation for the particular order;

+ knowledge about the order and its obligations;

+ integral faith, right intention, required knowledge, good reputation, good morals, proven virtues, other physical and psychological qualities appropriate to the order.

Men destined for the presbyterate are to be admitted to the order of diaconate only after they have reached the age of twenty-three, and to the presbyterate only after reaching the age of twenty-five. An interval of at least six months is to elapse between the reception of the two orders. Candidates to the permanent diaconate who are not married must be at least twenty-five, or thirty-five if married. A bishop may grant a **dispensation** of the age requirements for a younger candidate up to one year; the **apostolic see** is competent to grant a dispensation for more than one year.

One can be ordained to the transitional diaconate only after completing a five year curriculum of philosophical and theological studies. Candidates must have also completed a program of pastoral care while exercising diaconal ministry before ordination to the priesthood. A candidate for the permanent diaconate cannot be ordained until the proper formation has been completed.

Irregularities and Other Impediments (cc. 1040-1049)

Irregularities are formal canonical obstacles to receiving ordination or from exercising an order already received. These irregularities apply *whether or not* the person is even aware of them. The faithful are obligated to reveal to the ordinary or **pastor** any impediments to orders that they are aware of.

The following would be considered irregular for receiving orders:

✝ one who suffers under a form of insanity or some type of psychic disorder whom experts would judge incapable of correctly carrying out the ministry.

✝ one who has committed the ecclesiastical crime of **apostasy, heresy,** or **schism**.

✝ one who has attempted marriage, even a civil one, while impeded from entering marriage due to an existing marriage, sacred orders, or public perpetual vow of chastity, or who has attempted marriage with a woman who is bound by a **valid** marriage or by a perpetual vow of chastity.

✝ one who has committed voluntary homicide or has procured an effective abortion, or who has voluntarily cooperated in either.

✝ one who has seriously and maliciously mutilated himself or another person, or who has attempted suicide.

✝ one who has performed an act of orders reserved to an order he has not received, or who was forbidden to exercise the order due to an inflicted or declared penalty.

These irregularities must be dispensed by the proper authority. If the dispensation for an irregularity is not reserved to the holy see (see apostolic see) or is not presently being addressed in a judicial proceeding, it may be dispensed by the ordinary.

Impeded Simply (c. 1042)

Some are impeded simply from receiving orders. When the condition that impedes them has changed, the person can be eligible to advance to an order. The following are "simply impeded":

✛ a man with a wife, unless he is a candidate for the permanent diaconate.

✛ a person who holds a public office which involves a participation in the exercise of civil power or a secular office that would involve an obligation to render an account. Permanent deacons, however, are not bound by these prescriptions.

✛ a neophyte (one who has just been baptized), unless the ordinary judges him capable of receiving and exercising orders.

Irregularities for Those Already Ordained (c. 1044)

A person who has already received orders can be irregular for the exercise of those orders in the following cases:

✛ one who received orders when he had an irregularity.

✛ one who has publicly committed apostasy, heresy, or schism.

✛ one who has attempted marriage, even civil marriage, after receiving orders.

✛ one who has committed voluntary homicide or procured an effective abortion, or who positively cooperated in either.

✛ one who seriously and maliciously mutilated himself or another person, or who attempted suicide.

✛ one who exercises an act of orders reserved to an order he has not received or had been forbidden to exercise the order by virtue of some declared or inflicted penalty.

Impeded From Exercising Orders (c. 1044, §2)

The following would be *impeded* from exercising their order until the condition that prevents their exercise has been changed:

A Concise Guide to Canon Law

✛ one who has illegitimately received orders due to an irregularity present at the time of ordination.

✛ one inflicted with insanity or some other psychic defect which would in the opinion of experts make the person incapable of exercising orders. The person is impeded from exercising the order until the ordinary after consulting an expert, grants permission.

Registration and Certification of Ordination (cc. 1053, 1054)

After the ordination, the names of those ordained, the name of the ordaining bishop, and the place and date of the ordination are noted in a special register in the diocesan **curia**; in addition, the ordained is to receive some certification of ordination. The **local ordinary** (or in the case of religious, the competent major superior) is to send to the pastor of the place where the newly ordained was baptized, notification of the ordination to be recorded in the baptismal register.

1. *What is the difference between a "transitional" deacon and a "permanent" deacon?*

The permanent diaconate was restored by the Second Vatican Council. Up to the fifth century, the diaconate flourished in the Western Church, but after this period it experienced a slow decline, and survived only as an intermediate stage for candidates preparing for ordination to the priesthood. The Council of Trent had hoped to restore the permanent diaconate to its original function in the church, but this never materialized. With the apostolic letter *Sacrum Diaconatus Ordinem* of June 18, 1968, general norms were issued for a restored permanent diaconate in the Latin Church. Candidates for the permanent diaconate may be married or single, and undertake a "ministry of service" in a variety of settings, e.g., parishes, hospitals, relief organizations, etc. Although the church still requires that candidates for the priesthood must have received the diaconate, the role and understanding of the order is seen more clearly as "a proper and stable rank of the hierarchy" (*Vatican Congregations for Clergy and Education*, "Permanent Diaconate," Feb. 22, 1998).

Men may be admitted to the transitional diaconate at the age of twenty-three. To be admitted to the permanent diaconate a man must be at least twenty-five if single, thirty-five if married and with the consent of his wife. Formation and training for the transitional and permanent diaconate also vary accordingly.

2. *May a permanent deacon re-marry after his spouse has died?*

Canon 1087 legislates that any person in holy orders invalidly attempts marriage. Therefore, if the wife of a permanent deacon should die, he may not re-marry. In a circular letter of June 6, 1997, the Congregation for

Divine Worship and Discipline of the Sacraments addressed this issue. The letter mentioned the grave difficulties that have been reported concerning permanent deacons who have been widowed after ordination and are desirous of remaining in the diaconal ministry. One of three conditions may now be considered sufficient for a favorable consideration of a request for a dispensation from c. 1087: 1) "The great and proven usefulness of the ministry of the deacon to the diocese to which he belongs"; 2) "children of such a tender age as to be in need of motherly care"; 3) "parents or parents-in-law who are elderly and in need of care" (#8).

3. *May a priest ever be removed from the clerical state?*

Ordination to the priesthood, once validly received, never becomes invalid. Once ordained to the priesthood, the powers of the sacrament can never be removed. However, clerics can lose the juridical status of the clerical state and the right to exercise the office. Canon 290 states that clerics can lose the clerical state by one of three ways: 1) by a judicial decision or an administrative **decree** which would declare the invalidity of an ordination received, e.g., ordination administered by a bishop who did not impose hands together with the prescribed prayer. Canons 1708-1712 outline the procedure that is followed to establish whether or not ordination was invalidly received; 2) by the legitimate infliction of the penalty of dismissal. Such a serious penalty could only be imposed for offenses that are specifically mentioned in the code, e.g., sacrilegious treatment of the eucharist. Such a penalty could be imposed only after an ecclesiastical judicial trial; 3) by a determination of the apostolic see, granted to priests only for the most serious reasons. Such a petition is normally prepared and presented through the ordinary of the cleric's incardination (either diocese or religious institute).

Marriage

The sacrament of marriage is that sacrament in which a covenant is established between a man and woman, creating a partnership of the whole of life. By its nature marriage is ordered toward the good of the spouses and the procreation and education of children. By virtue of baptism, the covenant has been raised by Christ to the dignity of a sacrament.

Important Principles

1. **Unity** and **indissolubility** are the essential properties of marriage, which obtain a special firmness in a sacramental marriage. (c. 1056)

2. Marriage is created by the **consent** of the parties, an act of the will in which a man and a woman who are capable according to law irrevocably give and accept each other in order to establish marriage. (c. 1057)

3. Any person not prohibited by law can enter into marriage. **Canon law** regulates marriage even if only one partner is Catholic. **Civil law** also has **competence** regarding the civil effects of marriage. (cc. 1058, 1059)

4. Whenever there is a doubt about the validity of a marriage, marriage is the presumption, until the contrary is proven. (c. 1060)

5. A **valid** marriage between baptized persons which has not been **consummated** is referred to as *ratified*; after the marriage has been consummated, it is *ratified and consummated*. If the spouses have cohabited after the celebration of the marriage, the marriage is presumed to have been consummated. An invalid marriage is called **putative** if it was celebrated in good faith by at least one of the parties, until both parties become certain of its nullity. (c. 1061)

The Pastoral Care of Marriage (cc. 1063-1072)

Each **pastor** has the responsibility to see that the community provides instruction and care for those in his **parish** preparing to celebrate marriage. This is to be provided by:

✛ preaching and appropriate catechesis.

✛ personal preparation of the couple about the duties of the married state; he must also see to it that nothing stands in the way of a valid and **licit** celebration. The faithful are obliged to reveal any **impediments** to marriage that they are aware of. The couple should be strongly encouraged to receive the sacrament of penance and eucharist before celebrating marriage. If a Catholic has not yet been confirmed and it is not without serious inconvenience, the person is to be confirmed before the marriage. **The conference of bishops** determines how the parties are to be examined concerning their freedom to marry.

✛ well-celebrated marriage liturgy. There are many guides available today that can assist the pastor and couple in the preparation of the marriage liturgy.

✛ assistance to those in the community already married, emphasizing the beauty and dignity of the marriage covenant.

Marriages That Require Permission of the Local Ordinary (c. 1071)

Unless there is a necessity, no one is to assist at the marriage of any of the following circumstances without the permission of the **local ordinary**:

✛ marriage of a transient (person who has no **domicile** or **quasi-domicile**).

✛ marriage which cannot be recognized by civil law (e.g., some civil jurisdictions forbid marriage involving a person with a venereal disease).

✛ marriage involving a person who is bound by natural obligations toward another party or children from a prior union.

+ marriage of a person who has notoriously rejected the Catholic faith. The local ordinary may not give permission until the Catholic party has made appropriate promises in regard to children born of this marriage (see p. 78).

+ marriage of a person bound by a **censure**.

+ marriage of a minor when the parents are unaware of it or are reasonably opposed to the marriage.

+ marriage to be entered by **proxy**.

Marriage Impediments (cc. 1073-1082)

Impediments are canonical "obstacles" to a valid and licit celebration of a sacrament. When an impediment is present it renders a person incapable of celebrating marriage validly. If the presence of an impediment can be proven publicly, i.e., in the "external forum," it is called a public impediment. If not, it is referred to as "occult." Only the supreme authority of the church can establish impediments in addition to the ones listed on pages 68-71. And, as will be indicated, certain impediments can be dispensed only by the holy see. Some impediments are of divine law and can never be dispensed. All other impediments can be dispensed by the local ordinary for all his subjects wherever they are staying as well as for all those who are present in his territory.

In a particular case, the local ordinary can prohibit the celebration of a marriage for his subjects wherever they are staying and for those present in his territory, but only for a certain time and for a serious reason and for only as long as the serious cause continues to exist.

In danger of death, the local ordinary can dispense from every ecclesiastical impediment for his subjects wherever they are and all within his territory, as well as the **canonical form** for marriage (see p. 71-72), with the exception of the impediment of the sacred order of the **presbyterate**. When the local ordinary cannot be reached, the pastor, priest, deacon, or properly **delegated** minister may also dispense from the same impediments. (The local ordinary is considered to be inaccessible if he can be reached only by telephone or telegraph.)

Sometimes the pastoral minister, in preparing to celebrate a wedding, discovers that an impediment is present and the ceremony is imminent, with no time to contact the proper authority to obtain a **dispensation** for the impediment.

In this situation, the local ordinary can dispense from all the ecclesiastical impediments (whether public or occult), with the exception of:

✛ impediment arising from sacred orders or from a public perpetual vow of chastity in a **religious institute** of pontifical rite.

✛ impediment of crime (p. 70).

✛ impediment of **consanguinity** in the direct line or in the second degree of the **collateral** line (p. 70).

Pastors, priests, deacons, and properly delegated ministers for marriage also may dispense, if the impediments are occult and the local ordinary cannot be reached, as above. Some local ordinaries extend this faculty to include public impediments as well.

This ability to dispense from impediments "when all is prepared" also may be extended to situations involving "**convalidation**" (pp. 73-74) of marriages as well.

The pastor or priest or deacon who grants the dispensation in the external forum under the above circumstances ("all is prepared") is to inform the local ordinary of this dispensation and make sure that the fact of the dispensation is recorded in the marriage register.

Specific Impediments

Age (c. 1083)

A man under sixteen years of age or a woman under fourteen years of age cannot validly enter into marriage.

Impotence (c. 1084)

Antecedent (before the marriage) and *perpetual* (on-going and continuing) *impotence* to have intercourse, whether in the man or woman, and whether absolute (always incapable) or relative (with this particular partner), invalidates marriage. If the presence of the impediment is doubtful, the marriage is not to be impeded nor to be declared null as long as the doubt exists.

PRIOR BOND (C. 1085)

A person who is held to the bond of a prior marriage (even if not consummated) invalidly contracts marriage. The person may not contract a new marriage until the invalidity of the prior marriage has been legitimately and certainly established.

DISPARITY OF CULT (CC. 1086, 1125, 1126)

Marriage between a baptized Catholic (or one who has been received into the Catholic Church) who has not left the church by a formal act, and a person who is not baptized, is invalid.

Before this impediment can be dispensed, the following conditions are necessary:

✦ The Catholic party must declare that he or she is prepared to remove dangers of falling away from the faith and make a sincere promise to do all in his or her power to have all children baptized and raised in the Catholic Church.

✦ The other party is informed at an appropriate time of these promises and is fully aware of the obligations of the Catholic party.

✦ Both parties are instructed in the essential ends and properties of marriage.

If at the time of marriage it was commonly presumed that one party was baptized or even if it was doubted, the validity of the marriage is presumed until it is proven that one party was not baptized and the other party was. A Catholic who wishes to marry a baptized member of another faith tradition must make the same promises as mentioned above. In this case, it is *permission* that is sought from the local ordinary, not a *dispensation* from an impediment. (Without a dispensation from an impediment the marriage is considered invalid; without permission it is valid, but illicit.)

SACRED ORDERS (C. 1087)

A person who has received sacred orders attempts marriage invalidly.

VOW OF CHASTITY (C. 1088)

A person who has publicly professed perpetual vows of chastity in a religious institute attempts marriage invalidly.

ABDUCTION (C. 1089)

A marriage attempted between a man and a woman who has been abducted is invalid, until the woman freely gives her consent after being released.

CRIME (CRIMEN) (C. 1090)

A marriage attempted by a person who for the purpose of marriage with a certain person brings about the death of that person's spouse, or one's own spouse, is invalid. A couple would also invalidly attempt marriage if they bring about the death of one of their spouses through mutual physical or moral cooperation.

CONSANGUINITY (RELATIONSHIP BY BLOOD) (C. 1091)

A marriage is attempted invalidly between a person and all descendants and ancestors in the *direct line* (parent, grandparent, son, grandson, etc.) whether the relationship is legitimate (through marriage) or natural. A marriage is also attempted invalidly in the *collateral line* (e.g., siblings, cousins, etc.) up to and including the *fourth degree* (first cousins). If there is a doubt about the relationship in the direct line or up to the second degree of the collateral line, marriage is never permitted.

AFFINITY (RELATIONSHIP BY MARRIAGE) (C. 1092)

Relationship by marriage in the direct line, **affinity** (e.g., a man and his second wife's daughter), invalidates an attempted marriage.

PUBLIC PROPRIETY (C. 1093)

An invalid marriage is attempted between a person who has established common life with another or lives in notorious or public concubinage, with a person who is of the first degree of the direct line (child or parent) of the partner (e.g., the daughter of the man's mistress). This impediment is referred to as *public propriety.*

An invalid marriage is attempted between one person and another who is *related by adoption* in the direct line or in the second degree of the collateral line (brother or sister).

Form for Marriage (cc. 1108, 1109, 1110, 1111)

Catholics are obliged to observe canonical form when they enter into marriage. By canonical form is meant that Catholics must marry in the presence of a properly delegated priest or deacon, and in the presence of two witnesses. The priest (or deacon) present must ask for the couple to exchange their consent in his presence. For a Latin Rite cleric to witness a marriage ceremony, at least *one* of the parties must be a Latin Rite Catholic. The cleric can validly assist at a marriage *only within his territory*. To assist at a marriage in another parish (even if one or both of the parties are his subjects), the cleric must receive delegation (conferring proper power to act upon a person who does not have the power by the proper authority) authorizing him to assist at the marriage, normally obtained from the pastor of the parish where the marriage is to be celebrated.

Dispensation From Canonical Form (c. 1127)

Sometimes, when it will be difficult to observe canonical form in a certain marriage ceremony, it is proper to seek a dispensation from form, so that someone other than a priest or deacon (e.g., a minister of another faith tradition) can assist at the marriage. This would be the case if one of the parties is not Catholic and the couple wishes to have the minister of the non-Catholic party witness the marriage. A dispensation from canonical form can be petitioned from the local ordinary. Usually an application form for this dispensation is provided by the local **chancery** which typically also includes on the same form a petition for a dispensation from the impediment for a Catholic marrying an unbaptized person or a petition for permission for a Catholic to marry a person baptized into a different faith. This application is made to the local ordinary of the Catholic party.

Before granting the dispensation from form, the local ordinary must consult the **ordinary** of the place where the marriage is to be celebrated (if it is to take place in another **diocese**) to see if there is any objection.

Also, for validity, it is *required* that there be some public form of celebration of this wedding.

In the case of a marriage between a Catholic and a non-Catholic of an oriental rite, the canonical form is observed only for liceity (see licit). It is necessary, however, for validity that a sacred minister be present along with the other requirements of law.

When a dispensation from form has been granted, only *one* exchange of consent is permitted. It is forbidden to have two different and distinct celebrations of consent (e.g., the Catholic minister asks for consent from the Catholic party, and the Protestant minister asks for consent from the Protestant party).

Contracting Marriage in the Presence of Witnesses Alone (c. 1116)

If it is impossible without serious inconvenience for a couple to exchange their consent in the presence of a person who is competent to witness their marriage, couples may contract marriage in the presence of witnesses alone:

✢ when in danger of death; or

✢ when it is seen that the circumstances of inaccessibility to a proper minister will continue for at least a month.

If a priest or deacon is readily available, he must be called to witness the marriage along with the witnesses.

Place for Marriage Celebration (cc. 1115, 1118)

The marriage of two baptized Catholics or a Catholic and another baptized person of another faith tradition is to be celebrated in a parish church. The local ordinary can give permission for the marriage to be celebrated in another church or **oratory** or in another suitable place. Marriages between a Catholic and an unbaptized person can be celebrated in a church or some other suitable place. The chancery should be consulted concerning any local legislation about the place for the proper celebration for marriages in the diocese.

Recording Marriages (cc. 1121-1123)

After the celebration of the marriage, the pastor of the place of the celebration of the marriage is to record in the marriage register, as soon as possible:

✛ the names of the spouses;

✛ the person who assisted (priest or deacon);

✛ the names of the witnesses;

✛ the date and place of the wedding.

If the wedding is to be celebrated with a dispensation from canonical form, the local ordinary is to see to it that the pastor of the Catholic party who conducted the pre-marital inquiry concerning the freedom of the parties inscribes the marriage information and dispensation into the marriage register. This is also recorded at the diocesan **curia**. The Catholic party is to notify the local ordinary and pastor as soon as possible after the wedding as to the place and the public form that was used.

The marriage is also to be noted in the baptismal register of the Catholic party (parties). This notation is also made whenever a marriage is convalidated (see "Convalidation of Marriage" below) in the external forum.

Secret Marriages (cc. 1130-1133)

Sometimes, for a serious and urgent reason, it may be necessary for a marriage to be celebrated secretly. Permission for such a marriage must be obtained from the local ordinary, who grants permission as well for the pre-marital investigation to be made secretly. The local ordinary, minister, couple, and witnesses must all observe secrecy concerning this celebration. The marriage is to be recorded in a special register in the secret **archives** of the diocesan curia.

The parties must be informed before the ceremony that the local ordinary is not held to secrecy if there would be serious scandal or serious harm to the sanctity of marriage if the secrecy of the marriage was maintained.

Convalidation of Marriage (cc. 1156-1160)

If a marriage is invalid due to an impediment, once the impediment no longer is present, or has been dispensed, it is possible to convalidate the wedding, providing that at least the partner aware of the impediment renews consent. This *renewal of consent* is necessary for convalidation even if both parties gave consent at the beginning of the marriage and did not revoke it.

If the marriage is invalid due to a lack of canonical form (p. 71) it is necessary that the marriage now be contracted using proper canonical form.

Sanations (cc. 1161-1165)

Sometimes it may be necessary or appropriate to convalidate a marriage that is invalid *without having either party renew their consent*. This is referred to as radical sanation, a "healing at the root," in which a competent authority convalidates the marriage if there were any impediments present or if canonical form was not observed.

✛ The convalidation occurs at the moment it is granted.

✛ It is retroactive to the time the marriage was celebrated (unless sometime else is expressly stated).

✛ Parties must intend to persevere in conjugal life.

✛ Consent of the parties must continue to exist.

✛ Sanation can be granted even if both parties are unaware of it, but should not be granted except for serious reasons.

Authority to Grant Sanations (c. 1165)

The **diocesan bishop** can grant a sanation for individual cases, even when there are several reasons for the nullity of the marriage. In the case of an impediment for a Catholic marrying an unbaptized person, the conditions for dispensation from this impediment (p. 69) must be fulfilled. In matters in which the dispensation from an impediment is granted by the **apostolic see**, the sanation must likewise be granted by the apostolic see. In cases in which an impediment of divine or natural law has ceased to exist (e.g., prior bond), such sanations must also be granted by the apostolic see.

1. *If a couple is living together, does canon law forbid them to be married?*

A conflux of rights coalesce in this pastorally trouble-some situation, one which has become more and more commonplace in recent times. It is Catholic belief that marriage is a natural right. Canon 1058 states that all persons who are not prohibited by law can contract marriage. Canon 843, §1 establishes that sacred ministers cannot refuse the sacraments to those who ask for them at appropriate times, are properly disposed, and are not prohibited by law from receiving them.

Many pastoral ministers believe that living together as a couple before marriage makes a couple ineligible to be married in the church, since in such a situation the couple would not be properly disposed to receive the sacrament of marriage. The new catechism, in describing "trial marriage," says those who engage in premature sexual relations with the intention of getting married later enter a relationship that can "scarcely ensure mutual sincerity and fidelity . . ." (#2390). "Human love does not tolerate 'trial marriages.' It demands a total and definitive gift of persons to one another"(#2391).

It is only the ordinary who can legitimately prohibit the marriage of a couple within his jurisdiction, and only in a particular case—and only for a time, for a serious cause, and only as long as the cause exists (c. 1077, §1). Before the pastoral minister would refer such a case to an ordinary, it would be hoped that the marriage prepa-ration required by c. 1063 would give the pastoral min-ister the opportunity to engage the couple in an extensive "teachable moment." The Pontifical Council for the Family, in its document "Preparation for the Sacrament of Marriage" (July 4, 1996), describes this evangelization as both a "maturation and deepening in the faith" (#2). This document also called for an intense "remote preparation" in which the family, school, and other formation groups assist in the development of respect for all authentic human values both in interpersonal and social relations, "with all this implies for the formation of character, self-control, and self-esteem, the proper use of one's inclinations and respect for persons of the other sex" (#22).

2. *Should a priest/deacon witness a wedding when the woman is pregnant?*

The condition of pregnancy does not *ipso facto* indicate that the person would not be properly disposed to enter into marriage. However, the pastoral minister should be prudent, in conducting the pre-marital investigation, in attempting to determine whether there is any external or internal pressure to marry. The presence of such lack of freedom could result in the lack of full consent at the time of marriage, thereby invalidating the marriage. The pastoral minister should also receive medical documentation confirming the pregnancy.

3. *How much time should be established for marriage preparation before the wedding actually takes place?*

Pastors of souls in accordance with c. 1063 are obliged to see to it that their own ecclesial community furnishes the **Christian faithful** assistance that the marital state is maintained in a Christian spirit. Such assistance includes providing personal preparation to parties preparing to celebrate marriage. The document "Preparation for the Sacrament of Marriage" (see Question 1 above) discusses remote, proximate, and immediate preparation for the celebration of marriage. "Proximate preparation" takes place during the engagement and generally coincides with the period of youth, and therefore relates to everything that pertains to the pastoral care of youth. Such preparation includes specific courses, opportunities to deepen the life of faith, instruction regarding the natural requirements of the interpersonal relationship between a man and a woman in God's plan for marriage, awareness regarding freedom of consent, the unity and indissolubility of marriage, and the correct concept of responsible parenthood (#32-49). The "immediate preparation" that takes place during the period of the engagement includes a synthesis of previous preparation, experiences of prayer (e.g., retreats), and suitable liturgical preparation—taking place through special meetings of a more intensive nature (#50).

Obviously such proximate preparation should not be rushed, to provide the engaged couple and the pastoral minister the opportunity to investigate these themes and topics in some depth. **Particular law** in each diocese normally regulates the amount of time required to fulfill pre-marital requirements before the marriage can be properly celebrated. Such time lines vary typically from six to eight months.

4. *Does canon law establish in which church—the bride's or groom's—the wedding is to be celebrated?*

Marriages are to be celebrated in the parish where either of the persons has a domicile, a quasi-domicile, or has established a month-long residence (see c. 1115).

5. *May a "Catholic" wedding be celebrated outdoors?*

Canon 1118 establishes the places where marriages should be properly celebrated. Marriage between Catholics or between a Catholic and a baptized non-Catholic party is to be celebrated in a parish church; with the permission of the local ordinary or pastor, it may be celebrated in another church or oratory. The local ordinary can permit marriage to be celebrated in some other suitable place. Marriage between a Catholic party and a non-baptized party can be celebrated in a church or in some other suitable place. While the clear preference of the Code is for marriages to be celebrated in churches, the local diocesan offices should be consulted about local policy and guidelines concerning the possibility of outdoor weddings.

6. *Must the non-Catholic wishing to marry a Catholic make promises concerning the baptism and religious upbringing of children before the wedding may take place?*

Contrary to prior legislation, it is now the Catholic party who, before entering into marriage with a member of another church or ecclesial community, must obtain the permission of the local ordinary by making certain declarations about his or her faith (cc. 1124, 1125). Such permission may be given by the ordinary for a just and reasonable cause. The Catholic party must declare that he or she is prepared to remove dangers of falling away from the faith and make a sincere promise to do all in his or her power to have all children baptized and brought up in the Catholic Church. The other party must be informed of these promises made by the Catholic. Both parties must also be instructed on the essential ends and properties of marriage. Such a discussion would include the church's understanding of the community of love and life which is marriage, and the Catholic understanding of the purpose of marriage and the properties of indissolubility and fidelity. The impediment of "disparity of cult" exists for the marriage of a Catholic to a person who is not baptized (c. 1086); the above conditions must likewise be fulfilled before the impediment may be dispensed by the proper ordinary.

7. *May a non-Catholic minister preside at a marriage when a Catholic marries someone not of the Catholic faith?*

The local ordinary has the right, in individual cases, to dispense from the observance of canonical form (a properly delegated priest or deacon and two witnesses) and to allow a non-Catholic minister or civil official to receive the exchange of consent when a Catholic marries someone not of the Catholic faith (see c. 1127, §2). The proper ordinary to grant such a dispensation is the ordinary of the Catholic party—where the Catholic has a domicile or a quasi-domicile. If the marriage is to take place in another diocese, the local ordinary of that diocese must be notified that the dispensation has been granted.

8. *May a Catholic couple who has been married "outside the Church" have their marriage "convalidated"?*

It sometimes happens that a Catholic enters into marriage without following canonical form (i.e., in the presence of a properly delegated priest or deacon) or with an impediment present. The couple may wish to regularize their situation with the intervention of the church's minister. A *convalidation* (sometimes incorrectly referred to as a "blessing") of the marriage may take place. This happens by the couple renewing their consent according to proper canonical form. In the case of an impediment, the impediment must be dispensed or be no longer present before the consent may be renewed. Another manner of convalidation is sometimes employed, called *sanation*. This is done by the action of the bishop or holy see (or the one properly delegated by either), making the consent valid, and does not require the renewal of consent by either of the parties. Such a procedure can only be used when it appears certain that the original consent of the couple continues.

9. *Must a Catholic be confirmed before he or she may be married in the church?*

According to c. 1065, §1, if they can do so without serious inconvenience, Catholics who have not yet received the sacrament of confirmation are to receive it before being admitted to marriage.

Parishes

A parish is a definite stable community established within a particular church whose pastoral care is given to a pastor under the authority of the diocesan bishop. A quasi-parish is equivalent to a parish but as of yet has not been erected as a parish. Parishes are normally erected territorially, i.e., with geographical boundaries, but may be designed according to other factors, such as language or nationality, etc. Also, if circumstances require it, due to a dearth of priests, the diocesan bishop may assign participation in the pastoral care to deacons, or to someone else who is not a priest. There must, however, be a priest assigned by the diocesan bishop with the faculties of a pastor to supervise the pastoral care.

Pastor (cc. 515, 517, 521, 528-530, 534)

A **pastor** is assigned by the bishop to provide pastoral care for a **parish** community. A pastor must be an *ordained priest*. He is to have the care of only one parish, but due to a *dearth of priests* in a particular area, the bishop may assign him the care of several neighboring parishes. The **diocesan bishop** may also appoint a *team of pastors* to oversee the pastoral care of a particular parish or several parish communities, but one must be appointed *moderator*, with ultimate accountability to the diocesan bishop.

The responsibilities of a pastor include:

✛ preaching the word of God;

✛ sacramental celebration;

✛ fostering works in the spirit of the gospel, including social justice issues;

✛ providing for the Catholic education of children and young adults;

✛ outreach to those who are no longer practicing their faith or who do not profess the Catholic religion.

In addition, the pastor must celebrate Mass for the people entrusted to his care each Sunday and holyday of obligation.

Certain functions especially assigned to the pastor are:

✛ administration of baptism;

✛ confirmation to those in danger of death;

✛ administration of viaticum and anointing of the sick as well as the imparting of the apostolic blessing;

✛ assisting at marriages;

✛ performing funerals;

✛ blessing the baptismal water during Easter season;

✛ presiding at the more solemn celebrations of the eucharist on Sundays and holydays of obligation.

A pastor ceases from his office when he is removed, transfers, or resigns for a just cause and the resignation is accepted by the diocesan bishop. A pastor may also cease from office when he has been appointed for a specific term which time has expired. In the United States, the National Conference of Catholic Bishops has determined that diocesan bishops may appoint pastors to a six-year term, with the possibility of renewing the term left to the discretion of the diocesan bishop.

Parochial Vicar (cc. 539, 540, 545, 546, 552)

A **parochial vicar,** who must also be a priest, can be assigned to a pastor, to assist in providing pastoral care. Parochial vicars are co-workers with the pastor and provide appropriate counsel, working under his authority. There should exist a spirit of cooperation in parish endeavors and programs between the pastor and the parochial vicar. The parochial vicar can be removed from office by the diocesan bishop or diocesan administrator for a just cause.

Sometimes the diocesan bishop appoints a parochial **administrator** to assist in the pastoral care of a parish. This can occur when a parish is *vacant* or a pastor for some reason is *not capable* of exercising his pastoral duties. A parochial administrator must be a *priest* and is not permitted to prejudice the rights of the pastor or harm parish goods. The parochial administrator must give an account to the pastor when his service is completed.

Pastoral Council (c. 536)

A **pastoral council** is a selected group of the **Christian faithful** within a parish who, with the pastor and those who also share in the pastoral care of the parish, give help in fostering pastoral activity. A variety of means are utilized in the various **dioceses** for the selection of members, including voting by the entire parish. The pastor presides over the pastoral council. Many councils have a member serve as chairperson and also provide for other officers, in accordance with the statutes. Pastoral councils may be established in a diocese only after the diocesan bishop has listened to the **presbyteral council** and it seems opportune to have them. Pastoral councils possess a *consultative vote* and follow the norms laid down for these councils by the diocesan bishop in each diocese.

Finance Council (c. 537)

Each parish must have a **finance council**, a gathering of Christian faithful in the parish who meet to assist the pastor in the temporal affairs and financial administration of the parish. Each diocese is to have norms concerning such councils.

1. *What formalities of law must a bishop follow in order to close a parish?*

   Many dioceses in the United States the last few years have inaugurated planning programs that seek to evaluate future needs and parishes. As a result of these studies, it often happens that some parishes are suppressed (or formally closed) and perhaps new parishes are created. Canon 515, §2 states that the diocesan bishop alone is competent to "erect, suppress or notably alter parishes." However, before he makes such changes, he is first to hear the **presbyteral** (priests') **council**. The presbyteral council should be well informed before such a meeting and provided appropriate documentation so that the members may give good counsel when asked by the bishop. Also, should a church for serious reasons no longer be needed for divine worship, the diocesan bishop can relegate it to secular but not unbecoming or entirely inappropriate use after hearing the presbyteral council and obtaining the consent of those who claim legitimate rights to the church. Such a change must not impair the good of souls (c. 1222, §2).

2. *Must every parish in a diocese have a pastoral council? a finance council?*

   In accordance with c. 536, §1, after the diocesan bishop has listened to the presbyteral council and if he judges it opportune, a pastoral council is to be established in each parish. The pastor presides over it and parishioners along with parish staff assist in fostering parish activity. The pastoral council possesses a consultative vote and operates under norms approved by the diocesan bishop. Canon 537 requires a finance council in every parish made up of Christian faithful, regulated by universal norms as well as those of the diocesan bishop. Some responsibilities might include assistance in the preparation of the parish budget, assistance in the administration of parish temporal goods, and advice to the pastor in regards to parish fund-raising.

3. *May a deacon or a lay person ever be the pastor of a parish?*

In order to be appointed a pastor it is required that the person be an ordained priest (c. 521, §1). In addition, the person should be distinguished for sound doctrine, and endowed with a zeal for souls and other virtues, as well as those qualities that are established in universal and **particular law**. The church in the United States the last few years has struggled to provide pastors in many dioceses where there is a severe shortage of priests. Since 1983 and the revised *Code*, there is a new opportunity provided for the laity to assist in the pastoral care of a parish. Canon 517, §2 discusses the situation where there is a dearth of priests; the bishop may appoint a deacon, religious, or lay person, or a community of persons, to exercise pastoral care for a parish community. A priest, however, must be appointed with the "powers and faculties of a pastor, to supervise the pastoral care."

4. *How and in what circumstances may a bishop remove a pastor from a parish?*

If a pastor has been legitimately appointed to a term and the term has expired, the pastor can be reassigned. When the ministry of a pastor has become detrimental or ineffective for any reason, even if it not be due to any grave cause of his own, he can be removed from the parish by the diocesan bishop (c. 1740). Canon 1741 mentions five generic reasons that could prompt removal:

1. a way of acting which is gravely detrimental or disturbing to the ecclesial community;

2. incompetence or a permanent infirmity of mind or body which renders the pastor incapable of performing his duties;

3. loss of good reputation among upright and good parishioners or some aversion to the pastor by the

parishioners which is foreseen as lasting for some time;

4. grave neglect or violation of parochial duties which continue after a warning;

5. poor administration of the temporal affairs of the parish with grave damage to the church which cannot be handled in any other way.

The bishop, in order to remove the pastor, must carefully observe the procedure for the removal of a pastor outlined in canons 1740-1747, which include the conducting of an inquiry; discussion of the situation by the bishop with two pastors from a group permanently selected for this by the presbyteral council from a list nominated by the bishop; paternally persuading the pastor to resign the pastorate within a period of fifteen days, with the reasons and arguments for removal; repeat of the bishop's invitation for the pastor's resignation. If the pastor refuses to respond within the time limit or refuses to resign with no reason offered, the bishop may issue a **decree** of removal. If the pastor opposes the causes alleged for removal and gives reasons for remaining which seem insufficient to the bishop, the bishop invites the pastor to prepare a defense in a written report and offer proofs to the contrary. The bishop must allow the pastor to review the acts of the case that have been prepared against him. The bishop must consider the matter with the same two priests selected from the presbyteral council and then finally determine whether the pastor must be removed, promptly issuing a decree on the matter. The bishop must provide for the priest removed by providing him with assignment to another office (if he is suitable for this) or through a pension as the case requires and circumstances permit. Should the priest decide to make a formal appeal to the holy see against his removal, the bishop may not appoint a new pastor, but instead must appoint a parish administrator, pending the outcome of the appeal.

The Diocesan Church

A diocese is the portion of the people of God united by the Holy Spirit through the gospel and the eucharist, entrusted to a bishop for pastoral care, with the cooperation of the presbyterate. It constitutes a particular church where the one, holy, catholic and apostolic church is truly present.

Diocesan Bishop (cc. 376, 377, 383, 386, 388)

Bishops have general responsibility for the governance of the **diocese** and are appointed to this task by the pope. Bishops are called *diocesan* when they exercise pastoral care for the entire diocese. Other bishops are called *titular*.

Among the many responsibilities of a **diocesan bishop** are:

✛ preaching and teaching the gospel;

✛ coordinating various apostolates and ministries of the diocese;

✛ being concerned for all Catholics within the diocese;

✛ being concerned for those for whom ordinary pastoral care is not available;

✛ being concerned for those who do not practice their faith;

✛ providing pastoral care for those of different rites within his diocese;

✛ expressing kindness and charity to those not in full communion with the Catholic Church;

✛ being concerned for those not baptized;

✛ attending to the presbyters with special concern;

✛ fostering vocations to different ministries and to consecrated life through homilies proclaiming the good news and explaining truths of the faith to all the **Christian faithful**;

+ applying Mass for the people of his diocese on Sundays and holydays of obligation;

+ presiding frequently over the celebration of the eucharist.

The Diocesan Synod (cc. 460-468)

A **diocesan synod** is a gathering of selected priests and other Christian faithful of the local church in order to give assistance to the diocesan bishop for the welfare of the entire diocese. The bishop must first consult with the **presbyteral council** before convoking such an assembly.

The following must be invited to attend a diocesan synod:

+ **coadjutor bishop** and **auxiliary bishop**(s);

+ **vicar**(s) **general, episcopal vicar**(s), **judicial vicar**;

+ presbyteral council;

+ lay members of Christian faithful selected by diocesan **pastoral council** in manner determined by diocesan bishop; if no pastoral council, in a manner determined by diocesan bishop;

+ rector of diocesan major seminary;

+ **vicar**(s) **forane**;

+ at least one priest from each pastoral region (or zone) of the diocese selected by the priests of that area who exercise pastoral care;

+ some superiors of **religious institutes** and **societies of apostolic life** who have houses in the diocese, in a manner determined by diocesan bishop;

+ observers from other faith traditions, if the bishop deems opportune;

+ other clerics, members of consecrated life, or laity.

A diocesan synod should provide opportunity for a free discussion of the important questions and issues that make up the agenda. However, the bishop, as chief legislator for the diocese, signs any legislative texts that are produced by the synod and **promulgates** them as law by his authority. He may dissolve or suspend the synod at any time.

The Diocesan Curia (cc. 469-474)

The diocesan **curia** consists of the institutions and people who assist the diocesan bishop in the governance of the entire diocese, especially in regard to the pastoral activities that make up the local church. Some members of the diocesan curia assist the bishop in providing administrative support; others in exercising judicial power (**tribunal**). Those who assist the bishop in the curia are to exercise their offices faithfully and to observe confidentiality as required. The bishop coordinates the offices and ministries that are exercised within the curia. However, he may appoint a moderator for this role, who should be a priest.

Vicar General (cc. 475-481)

A **vicar general** is a priest who is appointed by the diocesan bishop to assist him in the governance of the entire diocese. He must be at least thirty years of age, hold a doctorate or licentiate in **canon law** or theology (or at least be truly expert in these areas), and be of sound judgment. He is given **ordinary power** which he exercises in collaboration with the diocesan bishop. If he is not an auxiliary bishop, he is appointed for a certain term, or period of time which the bishop may freely renew. He may be removed from office by the diocesan bishop at any time. Unless he is an auxiliary bishop, a vicar general ceases from office when the diocesan bishop is no longer in office, due to death, transfer, or resignation.

Episcopal Vicar (cc. 476-481)

An episcopal vicar is a priest who assists the diocesan bishop in the governance of the diocese, in certain prescribed areas or in a particular matter or for a certain group of individuals or for a determined rite. The qualifications for an episcopal vicar are the same as for a vicar general (see above). However, his executive power is exercised only in those areas to which he is assigned by the diocesan bishop. If not an auxiliary bishop, he is appointed for a certain term, or period of time which the bishop may freely renew. He may be removed from office by the diocesan bishop at any time. Unless he is an auxiliary bishop, an episcopal vicar ceases office when the diocesan bishop is no longer in office, due to death, transfer, or resignation.

Chancellor (cc. 482-491)

The **chancellor** is appointed by the diocesan bishop to supervise the maintenance of the official documents of the curia and to oversee the diocesan **archive(s)**. The chancellor may be a lay person or cleric. The chancellor also serves as notary for official documents of the diocesan curia. The chancellor may be assisted by a vice chancellor. By custom, especially in the United States, chancellors have traditionally served in administrative capacities in the diocesan curia.

The diocesan archives contain the official instruments and writings concerning the spiritual and temporal affairs of the diocese. The diocesan archives must be secured and access is granted only by the bishop or by both the chancellor and moderator of the curia. Documents may not be removed except with the permission of the bishop or of both the chancellor and moderator of the curia.

Finance Officer (c. 494)

The bishop must appoint, *after listening to the* **consultors** *and finance council*, a **finance officer**, skilled in financial matters and distinguished by integrity. The finance officer is appointed to a five-year term (renewable) and assists the bishop in administering the temporal goods of the diocese and implements the budget that has been approved by the bishop and determined by the finance council. A financial report must be presented by the finance officer to the finance council at the end of every fiscal year. The finance officer can be removed by the diocesan bishop only for a grave cause and after he has consulted both the diocesan finance council and college of consultors.

The Diocesan Finance Council (c. 492)

A diocesan finance council is *necessary* in every diocese. It consists of at least three members of the Christian faithful, skilled in financial affairs as well as in **civil law**. They are appointed by the diocesan bishop for a five-year term (which may be renewed). They may not be related to the bishop up to the fourth degree of **consanguinity** or **affinity**. Included in their responsibilities is the preparation of a budget for the diocese. They also review at the end of the year the receipts and expenditures.

The Presbyteral Council (cc. 495-501)

The presbyteral council is a gathering of a body of priests of the diocese functioning somewhat like a senate to the bishop and who aid the bishop in the governance of the diocese. The bishop approves the statutes of this council. With regard to the designation of the members of the presbyteral council:

✛ about one-half are freely elected by the presbyterate.

✛ some are "ex-officio" serving on the council due to their office, e.g., a vicar general.

✛ the bishop is free to name other priests.

All secular priests incardinated into the diocese may vote for membership to the presbyteral council and are eligible for election in accordance with the statutes. Priests who are members of an **institute of consecrated life** or society of apostolic life may vote for membership to the presbyteral council and be eligible for election in accordance with the statutes. The rights to election may be extended to other priests who are not incardinated but have residence in the diocese.

The bishop determines the agenda for the council and can enlist matters for discussion from the council. This body is consultative to the bishop and he must consult with it in matters determined by law, such as:

✛ advisability of convoking a diocesan synod;

✛ modification of **parishes**;

✛ determination for use of offerings given by the faithful on the occasion of pastoral service to be placed in general common fund;

✛ appropriateness of establishing parish pastoral councils in the diocese;

✛ construction of a church or conversion of church to secular purposes;

✛ imposition of a diocesan tax.

When the see of the diocese is vacant, the presbyteral council ceases and its functions are assumed by the consultors (see page 92).

Consultors (c. 502)

The consultors are a body of priests selected by the bishop *from the presbyteral council* to constitute a "college" who perform certain functions determined by law. There must be at least six and not more than twelve consultors. They serve for a five-year term as a college. The bishop presides over the consultors. Some of their functions include:

✛ election of a diocesan administrator when the see is vacant;

✛ certain duties when the see is vacant;

✛ advising in regards to the hiring and firing of the diocesan fiscal officer;

✛ giving consent for acts of extraordinary administration (see p. 105);

✛ giving consent for certain acts of **alienation** of ecclesiastical property (see p.105).

1. *How often must a bishop convene a diocesan synod?*

   A synod is an opportunity for the particular church to gather to give assistance to the diocesan bishop for the good of the entire diocesan community. It is up to the bishop of the particular church to decide when circumstances warrant the gathering of the diocese in synod. However, before convoking a synod the bishop must have consulted with the presbyteral council (c. 461, §1).

2. *May lay people participate in a diocesan synod?*

   The synod is to consist of a group of selected priests and other Christian faithful of the local church (c. 460). Lay members, selected from the pastoral council in a manner and number to be determined by the diocesan bishop, are specifically required to attend; if no pastoral council (diocesan) exists, then the participation of the laity in the synod is to be in a manner determined by the diocesan bishop (c. 463, §1, 5°).

3. *Must a diocese have a diocesan finance council? a diocesan pastoral council?*

   To assist the diocesan bishop in the administration of diocesan temporal goods and his oversight of the financial operation of the diocese, the 1983 *Code* requires the establishment of a diocesan finance council (c. 492). The bishop (or his delegate) presides over this consultative body, composed of at least three members of the Christian faithful who are to be skilled in financial matters as well as civil law and people of outstanding integrity. They are appointed to this position by the bishop. **Universal law** requires that they be consulted by the diocesan bishop in some important matters, such as the more important acts of administration (as well as consulting with the college of consultors). Sometimes the bishop even needs their consent, e.g., acts of extraordinary administration (c. 1277) as defined by the **conference of bishops**, along with the consent of the consultors. When the diocesan bishop is "alienating" diocesan property (selling or losing control of the property in some way) the diocesan finance council must give their consent when the value of the goods alienated is within a certain minimum and maximum amount determined by the conference of bishops. The present approved minimum and maximum amounts in the United States are $500,000 to $3,000,000. If the value of the goods to be alienated is over $3,000,000 it requires, in addition, the approval of the holy see.

From the Second Vatican Council's emphasis on the participation of the laity in the life of the church comes the development of the diocesan pastoral council. This consultative body consists of Christian faithful who are in full communion with the Catholic Church—clerics, members of institutes of consecrated life, and especially lay persons—all designated for this council in a manner determined by the diocesan bishop (c. 512, §1). Their role is to investigate all those things that pertain to pastoral works, to reflect on them, and then to propose practical solutions. The existence of such a body in a diocese is to the extent that "pastoral circumstances recommend it" (c. 511). The diocesan pastoral council enjoys a consultative vote (c. 514, §1). It is to be convoked once a year (c. 514, §2) and ceases to function when the see is vacant (c. 513, §2).

4. *Who has responsibility for preparing the diocesan budget?*

Canon 493 specifies that the diocesan finance council is to prepare each year, according to the directions of the diocesan bishop, a budget of the income and expenditures foreseen for the governance of the entire diocese in the coming year. In addition, at the close of the fiscal year, the finance council is to examine a report of the receipts and expenditures (c. 493), as provided by the diocesan fiscal officer. It is the responsibility of the diocesan fiscal officer to administer the goods of the diocese in accordance with the budget that has been determined by the finance council (c. 494, §3).

5. *Are there any circumstances when a diocesan bishop must consult with his presbyteral council?*

The presbyteral council is a body of priests that advises the bishop in the governance of the diocese. Some of the members are elected by the presbyterate of the diocese, while others are *ex-officio* and serve on the council by virtue of their office in the diocese, according to the statutes for the council approved by the bishop. There are seven specific matters for which the bishop must consult with the presbyteral council:

1. Whether or not to conduct a diocesan synod (c. 461, §1).

2. Whether to erect, suppress, or notably alter a parish (c. 515, §2).

3. In order to make a determination about the allocation of offerings from the Christian faithful given on the occasion of services (c. 531).

4. Whether or not to establish pastoral councils in the diocese (c. 536).

5. Whether or not to construct a new church (c. 1215, §2). He must also consult with the rectors of neighboring churches.

6. Whether or not to convert a church to secular (but not sordid) use for reasons other than its poor condition. It is further required that the bishop obtain the consent of those who legitimately claim rights regarding the church (c. 1222, §2).

7. Whether to impose a moderate tax for diocesan needs on public juridic authorities subject to him. This requires in addition, consultation with the diocesan finance council. He can impose an extraordinary and moderate tax on other public juridic persons, but with the condition that it is a grave necessity and with the same consultation (c. 1263).

In addition, the presbyteral council must assemble a stable group of **pastors** from a list presented to them by the bishop, to be used in the procedures for the transfer or removal of a pastor.

Declaration of Invalidity (Annulment)

It sometimes happens that a party (or parties) to a marriage will approach the church through a marriage tribunal believing that the marriage is invalid and asking for a judgment about its validity. Many times it is the hope of one of the parties that he or she might enter another marital union. Often these people come to a parish minister seeking assistance in preparing the case that must be submitted to the tribunal.

Elements of Procedure

The following is an overview of the elements of the procedure that is followed. However, the local **tribunal** should be contacted in regard to local implementation of the procedures.

1. *Libellus* (petition seeking a determination concerning the validity of the marriage) is presented to the tribunal. (c. 1502)

2. The judge either accepts or rejects the petition after examining it to determine whether or not the court has **competence** to decide the case. (c. 1505)

3. The other party to the case, the respondent, is cited, so that he or she may participate in the case. (cc. 1507, 1508)

4. After consulting with both parties in the case, the judge is able to *formulate the doubt,* or delineate the issues and make some determination as to whether there will be proofs available to make a judgment. It is at the "joinder of issues" that some determination is made about the grounds on which the validity of the marriage will be judged. (cc. 1513-1516)

5. Proofs and witnesses are utilized by the tribunal to help the judge(s) come to a conclusion about validity of the marriage. (cc. 1526-1529, 1547-1573)

6. The parties and their advocates are invited to inspect the acts (proceedings) of the case at the tribunal. If there is legitimate concern that some serious danger would evolve from this inspection, the judge may decide that a certain act is not to be shared with the parties. The judge must not, however, jeopardize the right of defense. (c. 1598)

7. Parties declare nothing to add, the judge determines an appropriate time for the advocates to make pleadings for the case, time for proposing proofs expires, or judge declares proofs sufficiently instructed. (c. 1599)

8. The **defender of the bond**—a court officer—intervenes to propose in favor of the marriage bond, after carefully reviewing the case. (cc. 1432, 1602)

9. The judge (or, in some cases, a three-judge panel) makes a determination as regards the validity of the marriage. (cc. 1607-1610)

10. The sentence (judgment) is published, i.e., distributed to the parties, along with the means of appealing the sentence. (cc. 1611-1618)

11. The sentence, if affirmative, along with any appeals and the acts of the case, are sent to an appellate tribunal for confirmation of the sentence, or it may admit the case for a new trial if it is unable to confirm the first sentence. (c. 1682)

Possible Causes for Declaring a Marriage Invalid

There are three possible causes for declaring a marriage invalid:

✛ presence of **impediment**;

✛ lack of **canonical form**;

✛ defect of **consent**. Consent makes the marriage.

The law presents several possible areas in which consent may be lacking:

✛ some incapacity such as lacking use of reason, suffering from some grave lack of discretion of judgment, or inability to assume the essential obligations of marriage due to causes of a psychic nature. (c. 1095)

✛ ignorance that marriage is a permanent union between a man and a woman, ordered to the procreation of children through sexual cooperation. (c. 1096)

✛ error concerning the person married or an error about a quality of the person that was directly and principally intended. (c. 1097)

✛ marriage entered by fraud about some quality of the other person that by its nature would seriously disturb conjugal life. (c. 1098)

✛ error about the **unity, indissolubility**, or sacramental dignity of marriage which has determined the will. (c. 1099)

✛ simulating the marriage—giving the external appearances that consent was being given, while internally, by an act of the will, excluding marriage or some essential element or property of marriage. (c. 1101)

✛ entering marriage on the basis of a future condition. (c. 1102)

✛ marriage entered into by force or grave fear, from outside the person, making marriage the only viable way to be free of the fear. (c. 1103)

Officers of the Court

Judicial vicar: priest appointed by the bishop to exercise judicial power in his name. (c. 1420)

Judge: person appointed by the bishop to review cases submitted to the tribunal for determination concerning validity of marriage, after carefully studying the case. Judges may be clerics or laypeople. However, a lay judge can only exercise this office with a collegiate tribunal, i.e., with at least two other judges who are clerics. A judge must have a doctorate (or at least a licentiate) in **canon law**. (cc. 1446-1457)

Defender of the bond: a person appointed by the bishop to serve in the tribunal to "defend the bond." The defender must have a doctorate (or at least a licentiate) in canon law. In each case, the defender reviews the acts of the case and upholds the validity of the marriage bond. (c. 1432)

Assessor: a member of the tribunal who works as consultor to the judge and assists as needed.

Ponens: in a collegiate tribunal (when at least three judges are used), the ponens is the judge who writes the decision for the case. (c. 1429)

Auditor: member of tribunal who collects the proofs according to mandate of the judge. (c. 1428)

Notary: signs and authenticates acts of the case. (c. 1437)

Dissolution of the Bond (cc. 1141-1150)

A **ratified** and **consummated** marriage cannot be dissolved by any human power. There are some circumstances in which the marriage bond can be dissolved:

Non-consummated marriage: a marriage entered into by two baptized persons or between a baptized person and a non-baptized person can be dissolved by the Roman pontiff for a just cause at the request of one or both parties.

Pauline privilege: a marriage entered into by two non-baptized persons is dissolved in *favor of the faith* when a new marriage is contracted by one of the parties who receives baptism, provided the non-baptized person departs. The non-baptized person is considered to have "departed" if he or she does not wish to cohabit in peace with the baptized party or without insult to the Creator, unless after baptism the baptized person gave the other party just cause to depart. Before the baptized party can contract a new marriage, the non-baptized person is to be interrogated concerning:

✛ whether he or she wishes to be baptized;

✛ whether he or she wishes to cohabit in peace with the baptized party without insult to the Creator.

Since 1920, there have been cases in which dissolution of the bond was granted where one of the parties was baptized at the time of the marriage. Such a marriage is dissolved in "favor of the faith" when the parties desires to become Catholic or desires to marry a Catholic.

1. *Are children born of a union that is later declared invalid considered illegitimate?*

Canon 1061, §3 discusses the situation of an invalid marriage that has been entered into by at least one of the partners in good faith. Such a marriage is referred to as "**putative**." It may be invalid due to the presence of an impediment that has not been dispensed or a defect of consent. In a putative marriage, it is presumed that at least one of the partners gave consent in good faith. Canon 1137 states that children born of a putative marriage are considered legitimate.

2. *Must a non-Catholic whose marriage ends in divorce obtain an ecclesiastical annulment before he or she can marry a Catholic in the Catholic Church?*

The requirements of canon law concerning proper canonical form (being married in the presence of a properly **delegated** priest and two witnesses) apply only to Catholics. Therefore, the church would recognize as **valid** those marriages celebrated in other faith traditions as well as civil marriages, until the contrary is proven. The non-Catholic previously married and divorced wishing to marry a Catholic would need to submit his or her case to the diocesan tribunal. Many of these cases, similar to Catholics seeking a declaration of nullity, are petitioned on the basis of a defect of consent.

3. *Must the former spouse of a petitioner in an annulment proceeding be contacted?*

The procedure to establish the invalidity of a marriage is a tribunal procedure that follows a formal, legal process. It involves testimony, witnesses, and possible use of experts giving testimony, all leading to a decision made with moral certitude by an ecclesiastical judge or judges. Since the invalidity must be proven (marriage enjoys the favor of the law—when a doubt exists the validity of the marriage is to be upheld until the contrary is proven—c. 1060), the other partner to the marriage, the respondent, must be contacted. Obviously the declaration of nullity would also have consequences for the respondent as well. Immediately after the petition (libellus) has been submitted by the party seeking a declaration of nullity, the judge issues a citation to the respondent to participate in the process. Sometimes, after all efforts to locate a respondent have been exhausted, or the respondent refuses to cooperate in the procedure, the judge may rule to continue the tribunal proceeding (c. 1592, §1).

4. *Must a party pay in order to receive a declaration of nullity?*

To cover the costs that are incurred in conducting a declaration of nullity procedure, most tribunals have established a fee schedule. In most **dioceses**, it is the diocese itself that provides most of the subsidy for the tribunal. Those who can afford to pay are asked to make a contribution to the costs of operating an office, secretarial expenses, etc. Such fees have no bearing on the result of the procedure. Nor may someone be refused an opportunity to apply for a declaration when they are unable to pay. Many tribunals make adjustments in fees including a diminution of expenses for those who are truly unable to meet the fee schedule.

Temporal Goods

The church has the right to acquire, to alienate (or to dispose of), and to administer temporal goods. It utilizes temporal goods in many areas: churches are built for the celebration of the sacraments, buildings are erected for the appropriate ends of ministry, moneys are collected for the sustenance of the clergy and other pastoral workers and for the help that is needed by the poor. Goods that properly belong to the church are called "ecclesiastical" goods.

Acquiring Temporal Goods (cc. 1259-1272)

The church obtains or acquires temporal goods in a variety of ways:

✛ the faithful make contributions for the support of the church.

✛ **diocesan bishops** may impose a moderate tax for diocesan needs after hearing the diocesan **finance council** and **presbyteral council**.

✛ the **local ordinary** may prescribe the taking up of a special collection in all the churches for specific **parish**, diocesan, national, or universal projects.

Administering Ecclesiastical Goods (cc. 1273-1289)

Those who have responsibility for administering the temporal goods of the church must do so with care. Before administrators take office they must:

✛ take an oath before the **ordinary** or his delegate that they will be efficient and faithful administrators;

✛ prepare, sign, and subsequently renew an accurate and detailed inventory of movable and immovable goods, precious goods or goods of significant cultural value, or other goods, with description and appraisal. One copy of this inventory is maintained in the archives of the administration;

the other in the diocesan **archives** with any subsequent changes noted accordingly.

Responsibilities of All Administrators (c. 1284)

✢ Make sure that goods entrusted to their care are not lost or damaged and take insurance policies for these goods as necessary.

✢ Safeguard **ecclesiastical goods** through civilly **valid** methods.

✢ Observe both civil and **canon law** prescriptions or the intentions of the founder, donors, or lawful authority.

✢ Accurately collect revenue and income when legally due and safeguard them once collected.

✢ Pay interest on loans or mortgages when they are due and make sure that debts are paid on time.

✢ With consent of the ordinary, invest money left over after expenses have been met that can be profitably allocated for the purposes of the juridic person.

✢ Keep good financial books.

✢ Prepare an annual report at the end of each fiscal year.

✢ Arrange and deposit in the archives important documents and deeds and store a copy in the diocesan archives if convenient.

✢ Prepare an annual budget (strongly recommended).

✢ Under certain circumstances, make donations to charitable causes from their movable goods that do not belong to the stable patrimony.

✢ Observe meticulously **civil laws** in regard to labor and social policy in accordance with church principles in employment of workers.

✢ Pay employees a just and decent wage.

In addition, administrators are to give an account to the faithful of the goods that have been contributed. Administrators may not initiate a lawsuit or contest a suit without the written permission of their own ordinary.

The diocesan bishop must hear the finance council and the college of **consultors** in order to perform the more important acts of administration in the **diocese**. The **conference of bishops** is to determine *acts of extraordinary administration* that would require the consent of the diocesan finance council and the college of consultors.

Contracts and Alienation in Particular (cc. 1290-1298)

General and specific regulations concerning contracts and payments determined in the local area by civil law are to be observed in canon law with the same effects unless the civil law regulations are contrary to canon law or canon law makes some other provision(s).

It is necessary to obtain permission of the proper authority to validly alienate ecclesiastical goods according to the following criteria:

✛ When the value of goods to be alienated is between the minimum and maximum amount determined by the conference of bishops, it requires the permission of the diocesan bishop with the consent of the finance council, the college of consultors, and the parties concerned. If the juridic person is not subject to the bishop, the statutes of that juridic person make the determination as to what permission is required. Presently, in the United States, the limits are between $500,000 and $3,000,000.

✛ When the amount exceeds the maximum established by the conference of bishops, or goods donated by a vow to the church or goods that are especially valuable due to their artistic or historical value, it requires the permission of the holy see (**apostolic see**).

In order to alienate goods whose value is more than the minimum amount, it is necessary that there be a just cause and that there be a written estimate from experts concerning the value of the object to be alienated. Ordinarily, an object must not be alienated for a price that is less than the indicated estimate; any other prudent safeguards prescribed by legitimate authority are to be observed.

1. *May a pastor dispose of real property at any time?*

   The **pastor** represents the parish in all juridic affairs of the parish, in accord with the norms of law (c. 532). It is his responsibility to make sure that the goods of the parish are administered in accord with canons 1281-1288. Disposal of parish property ("**alienation**") is subject to the canons on alienation (1290-1298). If the value of the goods to be alienated is below what has been established by the conference of bishops as the range of minimum to maximum amounts that require the bishop to obtain consent from the consultors and diocesan finance council, it is the bishop who is the competent authority for alienation. Such transactions are also governed by civil law and the particular type of corporation that has been established for the diocese and the parish in a particular state. Most states have religious corporation laws that require the approval of the bishop before any transfer of church property may take place.

2. *Are there any restrictions on what financial acts a pastor may perform?*

   The acts of administration that a diocesan bishop may perform are regulated by c. 1277, which distinguishes between "more important acts of administration" which require that he listen to the finance council and the college of consultors, and "extraordinary acts of administration" which require that he obtain the consent of these same bodies. The diocesan bishop should issue particular norms for acts of administration that would be less than "more important acts of administration." Within these norms mention should be made of the limits for parish financial acts, as well as specification of what consultation may be required for a pastor to perform such acts, e.g., after consultation with the parish finance council.

3. *Are all contracts covered in civil law also bound by canon law?*

Canon 1290 qualifies the relationship between civil and canon law in the matter of contracts. Whatever general and specific regulations and payments are covered in contracts determined by civil law in a particular jurisdiction are observed by canon law with the same effects in matters that are subject to the governance of the church. The contracts are not acceptable in canon law, however, if the conditions are contrary to divine law or if canon law makes some other provision.

Rights in the Church

A dramatic development in the church since the Second Vatican Council has been the recognition of an array of rights for the Christian faithful. These flow from an appreciation of the true *equality of the Christian faithful, with all cooperating to build up the body of Christ in accord with each person's own condition and function. All rights are of course inseparable from obligations. Included among these rights and obligations of the Christian faithful are the following:*

Obligations and Rights of All the Christian Faithful (cc. 208-233)

✛ To maintain communion with the church. (c. 209)

✛ To live a holy life and to promote the growth of the church. (c. 210)

✛ To spread the gospel message. (c. 211)

✛ To follow the sacred **pastors** of the church, as teachers of the faith. (c. 212, §1)

✛ To make known their needs and desires to the pastors. (c. 212, §2)

✛ To manifest their opinion on matters that pertain to the good of the church to their pastors and other **Christian faithful**, with due regard to the integrity of faith and morals, with reverence to their pastors and consideration for the common good and respect for persons. (c. 212, §3)

✛ To receive assistance from pastors, especially the word of God and the sacraments. (c. 213)

✛ To worship God according to their own rite and follow their own spiritual life consonant with the teachings of the church. (c. 214)

✛ To found and govern charitable and religious associations or those that promote the Christian vocation in the world. (c. 215)

✛ To promote the mission of the church and to sustain apostolic action according to their own state and condition. (c. 216)

✛ To obtain a Christian education. (c. 217)

✛ To enjoy a freedom of inquiry and to prudently express opinions on matters in which they have expertise, while observing due respect for the magisterium. (c. 218)

✛ To be free from any coercion in choosing a state in life. (c. 219)

✛ To enjoy a good reputation and privacy. (c. 220)

✛ To legitimately vindicate and defend rights before a competent ecclesiastical tribunal; to be judged by law with equity; not to be punished except in accord with the norm of law. (c. 221)

✛ To assist with the needs of the church. (c. 222, §1)

✛ To promote social justice and to assist the poor. (c. 222, §2)

✛ To take into account the common good when exercising their rights which the competent authority can regulate. (c. 222, §§1, 2)

Obligations and Rights of the Laity (cc. 224-231)

✛ To work as individuals or in associations to spread the divine message of salvation. (c. 225, §1)

✛ To imbue the temporal sphere with the spirit of the gospel. (c. 225, §2)

✛ For those in the married state, to work to build up people of God through marriage and family; to educate their children, especially to provide a Christian education. (c. 226, §§1, 2)

✛ To exercise freedoms that are theirs within the society in which they live but to exercise their freedom imbued with the spirit of the gospel. (c. 227)

✛ When qualified, to assume positions and offices that they are able to exercise. (c. 228, §1)

✛ To assist pastors as experts or advisors in areas where qualified. (c. 227, §2)

A Concise Guide to Canon Law

+ To acquire knowledge of Christian doctrine, attend ecclesiastical universities, and obtain ecclesiastical degrees; to receive a mandate, when qualified, to teach the sacred sciences. (c. 229, §§1, 2, 3)

+ To be installed in the ministries of lector and acolyte (lay men only). (c. 230, §1)

+ To fulfill the functions of lector, commentator, cantor, or other functions on a temporary basis in accord with the prescriptions of law. (c. 230, §2)

+ When necessity warrants it and when ministers are lacking, to exercise the ministries of lector and acolyte even if not installed as such, in accordance with the prescriptions of law. (c. 230, §3)

+ To receive appropriate formation for whatever ministries they exercise for the church. (c. 231, §1)

+ To receive a decent remuneration, social security, and health benefits, when employed by the church. (c. 231, §2)

Glossary

Acta Apostolicae Sedis	The official publication of the holy see, containing papal decrees and any universal laws promulgated by the pope.
administrator (parish)	A priest who is appointed in a temporary capacity to perform the duties of a pastor in a parish.
affinity	The relationship between a spouse and all the relatives in the direct line of the other spouse.
age of reason	The age identified with obtaining the ability to make judgments about right or wrong, presumed to be the age of seven.
alienation	The juridical transfer, with or without compensation, of the ownership of property to another.
apostasy	Total repudiation of the Christian faith.
apostolic see (holy see)	A term that applies not only to the pope but also to the secretariat of state, and other institutions of the Roman curia, unless the nature of the matter or the context of the words makes the contrary evident.
archives (diocesan)	A place where diocesan records, documents, and various historical materials are maintained.

auxiliary bishop	The bishop who is appointed to assist the diocesan bishop in the governance of the diocese.
canon law	The official body of laws of the Roman Catholic Church. A systematic arrangement of the laws of the church occurred during the pontificate of Pope Pius X resulting in the *Code of Canon Law*. Pope John Paul II promulgated a new Code in 1983. In 1990 John Paul issued the *Code of Canons of the Eastern Churches*.
canonical form	The requirement that a Catholic be married in the presence of a properly delegated Catholic priest or deacon and two witnesses.
canonical penalty	A punishment that is placed on a person in accordance with law, for some violation of church law.
catechumenate	A spiritual and catechetical formation process in several stages that leads to initiation into the church.
censure	The canonical penalty of excommunication, or interdict or suspension.
chancellor	An official who must be appointed in every diocesan curia to see to it that the documents and records of the diocese are properly gathered, arranged, and safe-guarded.
chancery	Diocesan administrative offices.

chaplain	A priest to whom is entrusted the pastoral care, at least in part, of some community or particular group of the Christian faithful, to be exercised in accord with universal or particular law. He is to coordinate the exercise of his ministry with pastors.
chrism	A sacred oil, blessed by the bishop and used for anointing at baptism, ordination, confirmation, and the blessing of an altar.
Christian faithful	Those incorporated in Christ through baptism, constituted as the people of God, sharers in Christ's priestly, prophetic, and royal office.
civil law	The body of laws of a secular government.
coadjutor bishop	A bishop who aids the diocesan bishop in the governance of the entire diocese; he possesses the right of succession to the diocese.
collateral	The blood relationships between persons outside the direct line, such as siblings, cousins, aunts, etc.
competence	In an ecclesiastical tribunal, the proper jurisdiction of a certain tribunal to receive a case.
conference of bishops	A permanent institution consisting of the grouping of the bishops of a given nation or territory whereby, according to the norm of law, they jointly exercise pastoral functions on behalf of

the Christian faithful of their territory.

consanguinity	The blood relationship between people.
consent (marriage)	The action indicating the free choice or decision of one party to enter into marriage.
consultors (diocesan)	A permanent body selected by the bishop from the presbyteral council to advise him in certain matters; the college of consultors exercises certain functions of governance in the case of a vacant see.
consummated (marriage)	A marriage in which the partners have willingly and mutually performed the act of intercourse.
convalidation	An act of making valid the marriage consent that has been previously exchanged invalidly.
curia	Those institutions and persons that furnish assistance to the bishop (diocesan curia) or the pope (Roman curia), especially in regard to pastoral activity, administration, and in exercising judicial functions.
custom	A continued practice of people over an extended period of time. Under certain conditions, it can obtain the force of law.
decree	An administrative act issued by a competent executive authority in which a decision is given or a provision is made in a particular

	case in accord with the norms of law.
defender of the bond	An official of an ecclesiastical tribunal whose responsibility includes upholding the validity of the marriage bond in a marriage case.
delegated power	That power which is granted to a person but not by means of an office.
derogate	To diminish the strength of a law.
diaconate	The first order of the sacrament of holy orders, received prior to ordination to the priesthood (transitional diaconate). Since the Second Vatican Council, the permanent diaconate has been restored in which both single and married men are ordained to a ministry of service in the church.
dimissorial letter	A letter that testifies to suitability for ordination, presented to a bishop other than one's own.
diocesan bishop	A bishop with the care of a diocese; all others are titular.
diocesan synod	A formal gathering of selected priests and other Christian faithful of a diocese that offers assistance to the diocesan bishop for the good of the entire diocesan community.
diocese	A portion of the people of God that is entrusted for pastoral

A Concise Guide to Canon Law

care to a bishop with the cooperation of the priests.

dispensation
The relaxation of an ecclesiastical law in a particular case by
the competent authority.

domicile
The place where a person lives
for an indefinite time. In law it
is acquired by residence within
the territory of a certain parish
or at least of a diocese, which is
joined either with the intention
of remaining there permanently
unless called away or when the
person has actually lived there
for five complete years.

ecclesiastical goods
All temporal goods that belong
to the universal church, the
apostolic see, or other juridic
persons within the church.

ecclesiastical laws
As opposed to divine law from
God, those laws that are the cre-
ation of the appropriate church
authority.

episcopal vicar
A priest who possesses the same
ordinary power that universal
law gives the vicar general,
either in a determined section of
the diocese, over the faithful of a
determined right, over certain
groups of persons, or on a certain subject matter.

excardination
See incardination.

finance council
A group of the faithful at the
parish or diocesan level who
assist the pastor or bishop by
providing counsel in regard to

	financial matters of the parish or diocese.
finance officer (diocesan)	Appointed by the bishop, after listening to the college of consultors and the finance council, for a five-year renewable term. The finance officer administers the goods of the diocese under the authority of the bishop in accordance with the budget determined by the finance council and meets the expenditures that the bishop or others deputized by him have legitimately authorized.
general decrees	The means by which common prescriptions are issued by a competent legislator for a community capable of receiving a law; are laws properly speaking and are governed by the prescriptions of the canons on laws.
heresy	The obstinate post-baptismal denial of some truth that must be believed with divine and Catholic faith.
impediment (marriage)	A canonical barrier, some fact or condition in regard to a person that prevents the person from validly celebrating the sacrament of marriage.
incardination	The formal legal act of a cleric permanently attaching himself to an individual diocese or religious community. By means of *ex*cardination, a cleric formally separates himself from a diocese in order to join another.

indissolubility	An essential property of marriage indicating that the bond of marriage may never be dissolved or ended.
indult	A concession given for a certain period of time.
institute of consecrated life	A generic term for the form of life characterized by the profession of the evangelical counsels of poverty, chastity, and obedience.
instruction	A type of pronouncement from a Roman curial office that clarifies the prescriptions of laws and elaborates on and determines the approach to be followed in implementing them. An instruction is normally not a legislative document, in the sense that it does not create new norms.
irregularity	A canonical obstacle to ordination or the exercise of an order already received.
judicial vicar	A priest who possesses ordinary judicial power and who administrates the marriage tribunal.
law	An ordinance of reason for the common good, made by that person who has care for the community, and promulgated to that community (Thomas Aquinas).
licit	A canonical description of an act that has followed the prescriptions of law.

local ordinary	All those who are mentioned under category of "ordinary" except superiors of religious institutes and societies of apostolic life.
metropolitan	The archbishop of a diocese; he presides over an ecclesiastical province.
oratory	The place designated by the bishop as a site for divine worship for the use of a particular community or group of the faithful.
ordinary	A person who has been placed over a particular church or over a community that is equivalent to it, as well as those who possess ordinary general executive power in said churches and communities, namely vicars general and episcopal vicars; and likewise for their own members the major superiors of clerical religious institutes or pontifical right and of clerical societies of apostolic life of pontifical right, who possess at least ordinary executive power.
ordinary power (of governance)	That power which is joined to a certain office by the law itself.
Orientalium Ecclesiarum (Decree on the Eastern Churches)	A decree of the Second Vatican Council that promoted an understanding of and appreciation for the Eastern Churches and their liturgical rites and heritage.

Orthodox Churches	The Eastern Christian Churches that separated from full union with the Catholic Church.
parish	A definite community of the Christian faithful established on a stable basis within a particular church whose pastoral care is entrusted to a pastor as its own shepherd under the authority of the diocesan bishop.
parochial vicar	A priest appointed by the bishop to assist the pastor in the pastoral ministry of a parish; sometimes referred to also as "associate" or "curate."
particular law	A law that is promulgated in a specific territory, e.g., diocese, by the appropriate authority.
pastor	A priest who serves as the proper shepherd of a parish, exercising pastoral care under the authority of the diocesan bishop.
pastoral council	A group of the faithful at the parish or diocesan level who assist the pastor or the bishop by providing advice in regard to the pastoral work.
presbyteral council	A body of priests, like a senate of the bishop, representing the presbyterate, who aid the bishop in the governance of the diocese according to the norm of law in order that the pastoral welfare of the portion of the people of God entrusted to him may be promoted as effectively as possible.

presbyterate	The second order of the sacrament of holy orders, a priest who is not a bishop.
privilege	A favor given by a special act for the benefit of certain persons; it can be granted by the legislator and by the executive authority to whom the legislator has given the authority.
promulgate	To officially make a law; universal laws for the entire church are promulgated by the pope, normally by publication in the *Acta Apostolicae Sedis.* Diocesan laws or laws of an episcopal conference are promulgated through the means determined by the promulgating authority.
province	An ecclesiastical unit of the church consisting of a group of neighboring dioceses, with a metropolitan archbishop; a division by territory of a religious institute.
proxy (marriage)	A marriage in which at least one of the parties is represented by another person who has been officially designated by the party for this purpose.
putative (marriage)	An invalid marriage that has been entered into by at least one of the parties in good faith.
quasi-domicile	Residency within the territory of a certain parish or at least of a diocese that is acquired by the intention of remaining there at least three months unless called

	away, or by actual residency in the territory for three months.
ratified (marriage)	A valid marriage that has been entered into by two baptized persons.
religious institute	A religious order characterized by members who profess public vows of poverty, chastity, and obedience and who live a common life.
revoke	A general term for the power of a law or any legitimate authority to take away some right, privilege, or provision of law.
ritual church	One of the twenty-two churches that form the Roman Catholic Church: Latin, Ukrainian, Ruthenian, Melkite, Maronite, Armenian, Chaldean, Syrian, etc.
Roman curia	Congregations or offices in Rome through which the pope conducts the business of the universal church. The curia fulfills its duties in his name and by his authority for the good of and service to the church. Their structure and competence are defined in special law.
schism	Refusal of submission to the Roman pontiff or of communion with the members of the church subject to him.
seal of confession	Referring to the serious obligation for a confessor, under pain of excommunication, not to

reveal what has been heard in sacramental confession.

sede vacante

The vacant Roman see; a vacant episcopal see. An episcopal see is vacant upon the death of the diocesan bishop, upon his resignation accepted by the Roman pontiff, or upon transferal or deprivation of office made known to the bishop.

societies of apostolic life

Similar to religious communities, but the members, although living a common life, do not take vows.

synod of bishops

A group of bishops who have been chosen from different regions of the world and who meet at certain times to foster a closer unity between the Roman pontiff and the bishops, to assist the Roman pontiff by their counsel in safeguarding and increasing faith and morals and in preserving and strengthening ecclesiastical discipline, and to consider questions concerning the church's activity in the world.

titular see

A diocese that at one time flourished but presently is no longer in existence, except by name. Bishops without a residential diocese (e.g., auxiliary bishop) are assigned a titular see.

tribunal (diocesan)

Those courts established by the church to decide issues presented to it for resolution; most of the work of a tribunal involves cases presented for the determination of the invalidity of a marriage.

unity (marriage) An essential property of marriage that indicates complete monogamy and faithfulness.

universal laws Those laws that are established for the entire universal church, or for specific individuals within the entire church.

valid A canonical description that signifies that a particular act has its intended consequences due to its fulfillment of the requirements of the law.

vicar forane (Also called *dean* or *archpriest*) A priest who is placed over a vicariate, several parishes in a certain geographical area (sometimes referred to as a "deanery"). He is named by the bishop after consulting the priests who exercise ministry within the vicariate. He serves as a delegate of the bishop to the parish priests of his area.

vicar general The priest who assists the diocesan bishop in the governance of the entire diocese and who is endowed with ordinary power.

Suggested Reading

Abbo, J. and J. D. Hannon, *The Sacred Canons*, 2 vols., rev. ed. St. Louis, MO: B. Herder Book Co., 1957.

Alesandro, J., "Marriage and the Revised Code," in *New Catholic World*, 226 (1983), pp. 126-131.

Calvo, R. and N. Klinger, *Clergy Procedural Handbook*. Washington, DC: Canon Law Society of America, 1992.

Canon Law Society of Great Britain and Ireland, *The Canon Law Letter and Spirit: A Practical Guide to the Code of Canon Law*. Collegeville, MN: The Liturgical Press, 1995.

Caparros, E., M. Thériault, J. Thorn, eds., *Code of Canon Law Annotated*. Montréal: Wilson and LaFleur Limitée, 1993.

Cogan, P., *CLSA Advisory Opinions, 1984-1993*. Washington, DC: Canon Law Society of America, 1995.

Code of Canon Law: Latin-English Edition. Washington, DC: The Canon Law Society of America, 1983.

Coriden, J., *An Introduction to Canon Law*. Mahwah, NJ: Paulist Press, 1991.

_____, *The Parish in Catholic Tradition: History, Theology and Canon Law*. Mahwah, NJ: Paulist Press, 1997.

Coriden, J., T. Green, and D. Heintschel, eds., *The Code of Canon Law: A Text and Commentary*. Mahwah, NJ: Paulist Press, 1985.

Hite, J., and D. Ward, *Readings, Cases, Materials in Canon Law*, rev. ed. Collegeville, MN: The Liturgical Press, 1990.

Huels, J., *The Catechumenate and the Law: A Pastoral and Canonical Commentary for the Church in the United States*. Chicago, IL: Liturgy Training Publications, 1994.

_____., *The Pastoral Companion: A Canon Law Handbook for Catholic Ministry*. Quincy, IL: Franciscan Press, 1995.

Maida, A. and N. Cafardi, *Church Property, Church Finances, and Church-Related Corporations: A Canon Law Handbook*. St. Louis, MO: The Catholic Health Association of the United States, 1984.

McAreavey, J., *The Canon Law of Marriage and the Family*. Portland, OR: Four Courts Press, 1997.

McKenna, Kevin E. *The Ministry of Law in the Church Today*. Notre Dame, IN: University of Notre Dame Press, 1998.

Morrisey, F., *Papal and Curial Pronouncements: Their Canonical Significance in Light of the Code of Canon Law*. Ottawa: Faculty of Canon Law, St. Paul University, 1995.

Örsy, L., *Marriage in Canon Law: Texts and Comments Reflections and Questions*. Wilmington, DE: Michael Glazier Press, 1986.

Osborne, K., *Sacramental Guidelines: A Companion to the New Catechism for Religous Educators*. Mahwah, NJ: Paulist Press, 1995.

Pfnausch, E., ed., *Code, Community, Ministry: Selected Studies for the Parish Minister Introducing the Code of Canon Law*, 2nd rev. ed. Washington, DC: Canon Law Society of America, 1992.

Place, M., "A Guide to the Revised Code," in *Chicago Studies*, 23 (April, 1984), pp. 5-36.

Rinere, Elissa, ed., *New Law and Life: 60 Practical Questions and Answers on the Code of Canon Law*. Washington, DC: Canon Law Society of America, 1985.

Woestman, W., *Sacraments, Initiation, Penance, Anointing of the Sick*. Ottawa: St. Paul University, 1992.

Wrenn, L. G., *Annulments*, 4th ed. Washington, DC: Canon Law Society of America, 1983.

Rev. Kevin E. McKenna is Chancellor and Director of Legal Services for the Diocese of Rochester. Ordained in 1977, Fr. McKenna received his doctorate degree in canon law from St. Paul University in Ottawa in 1990. In addition to his current pastoral assignments as canonical consultant to the bishop and judge on the marriage tribunal, Fr. McKenna is a member of the Canon Law Society of America and the Canadian Canon Law Society. He is the author of numerous articles on canon law as well as the book *The Ministry of Law in the Church Today* (University of Notre Dame Press).